TEACHER'S PET PUBLICATIONS

LITPLAN TEACHER PACK
for
The Stranger
based on the book by
Albert Camus

Written by
Mary B. Collins

© 1996 Teacher's Pet Publications
All Rights Reserved

This **LitPlan** for Albert Camus'
The Stranger
has been brought to you by Teacher's Pet Publications, Inc.

Copyright Teacher's Pet Publications 1996
11504 Hammock Point
Berlin MD 21811

Only the student materials in this unit plan (such as worksheets, study questions, and tests) may be reproduced multiple times for use in the purchaser's classroom.

For any additional copyright questions,
contact Teacher's Pet Publications.

www.tpet.com

TABLE OF CONTENTS - *The Stranger*

Introduction	5
Unit Objectives	8
Reading Assignment Sheet	9
Unit Outline	10
Study Questions (Short Answer)	13
Quiz/Study Questions (Multiple Choice)	18
Pre-reading Vocabulary Worksheets	27
Lesson One (Introductory Lesson)	39
Nonfiction Assignment Sheet	41
Oral Reading Evaluation Form	43
Writing Assignment 1	50
Writing Assignment 2	52
Writing Assignment 3	54
Writing Evaluation Form	55
Vocabulary Review Activities	48
Extra Writing Assignments/Discussion ?s	47
Unit Review Activities	57
Unit Tests	61
Unit Resource Materials	89
Vocabulary Resource Materials	105

A FEW NOTES ABOUT THE AUTHOR
Albert Camus

CAMUS, Albert (1913-60). Living in a world overwhelmed by wars and political upheavals, Albert Camus believed that traditional human values must survive. While his novels, essays, and plays reflect an indifferent, meaningless universe, Camus argued the need to rebel against this absurdity-to defend such values as truth and justice.

Albert Camus was born on Nov. 7, 1913, in Mondovi, Algeria. Less than a year later, his father was killed in World War I. Camus studied philosophy at the University of Algeria, but his work was cut short by an attack of tuberculosis.

His first published works, collections of essays, describe his life in Algeria. Both collections contrast the fragile mortality of human beings with the enduring nature of the physical world. He wrote and acted for the Workers' Theatre, which aimed to bring outstanding plays to working-class audiences, and he worked as a journalist for the newspaper Alger-Républicain.

At the outbreak of World War II, Camus went to France, where he joined the Resistance movement and edited the Resistance newspaper Combat. His first novel, 'The Stranger', and an essay, "The Myth of Sisyphus," were published in French in 1942. His second novel, 'The Plague' (1947), is a symbolic account of the fight against an epidemic by characters who, while aware that their efforts are in vain, work on to try to ease the suffering of their fellow citizens.

In 1957 Camus received the Nobel prize for literature. On Jan. 4, 1960, he was killed in an automobile accident near Sens, France.

--- Courtesy of Compton's Learning Company

INTRODUCTION

This unit has been designed to develop students' reading, writing, thinking, and language skills through exercises and activities related to *The Stranger* by Albert Camus. It includes seventeen lessons, supported by extra resource materials.

The **introductory lesson** introduces students to one main theme of the novel through a class discussion prompted by Stephen Crane's *A Man Said to the Universe*. Following the introductory activity, students are given a transition to explain how the activity relates to the book they are about to read. Following the transition, students are given the materials they will be using during the unit. At the end of the lesson, students begin the pre-reading work for the first reading assignment.

The **reading assignments** are approximately thirty pages each; some are a little shorter while others are a little longer. Students have approximately 15 minutes of pre-reading work to do prior to each reading assignment. This pre-reading work involves reviewing the study questions for the assignment and doing some vocabulary work for 8 to 10 vocabulary words they will encounter in their reading.

The **study guide questions** are fact-based questions; students can find the answers to these questions right in the text. These questions come in two formats: short answer required or multiple choice-matching-true/false. The best use of these materials is probably to use the short answer version of the questions as study guides for students (since answers will be more complete), and to use the multiple choice version for occasional quizzes. It might be a good idea to make transparencies of your answer keys for the overhead projector.

The **vocabulary work** is intended to enrich students' vocabularies as well as to aid in the students' understanding of the book. Prior to each reading assignment, students will complete a two-part worksheet for approximately 8 to 10 vocabulary words in the upcoming reading assignment. Part I focuses on students' use of general knowledge and contextual clues by giving the sentence in which the word appears in the text. Students are then to write down what they think the words mean based on the words' usage. Part II nails down the definitions of the words by giving students dictionary definitions of the words and having students match the words to the correct definitions based on the words' contextual usage. Students should then have an understanding of the words when they meet them in the text.

After each reading assignment, students will go back and formulate answers for the study guide questions. Discussion of these questions serves as a **review** of the most important events and ideas presented in the reading assignments.

After students complete reading the work, a lesson is devoted to the **extra discussion questions/writing assignments**. These questions focus on interpretation, critical analysis and personal response, employing a variety of thinking skills and adding to the students' understanding of the novel.

Following the discussion session, there is a **vocabulary review** lesson which pulls together all of the fragmented vocabulary lists for the reading assignments and gives students a review of all of the words they have studied.

The **group activity** which follows the discussion questions has students working in small groups to discuss the main ideas of the novel. Using the information they have acquired so far through individual work and class discussions, students get together to further examine the text and to brainstorm ideas relating to the themes of the novel.

The group activity is followed by a **reports and discussion** session in which the groups share their ideas about the themes with the entire class; thus, the entire class is exposed to information about all of the themes and the entire class can discuss each theme based on the nucleus of information brought forth by each of the groups.

There are three **writing assignments** in this unit, each with the purpose of informing, persuading, or having students express personal opinions. The first assignment is to inform: students write a composition in which they prepare for the oral report they have to give relating to their nonfiction reading assignment. The second assignment is to persuade: students take the side of either the prosecution or defense of Meursault and write their closing arguments to the jury. The third assignment is to express personal opinions: after a discussion about responsibility, students write a composition in which they answer the question, "Are you a responsible person?".

There is a **nonfiction reading assignment**. Students are required to read a piece of nonfiction related in some way to *The Stranger*. After reading their nonfiction pieces, students will fill out a worksheet on which they answer questions regarding facts, interpretation, criticism, and personal opinions. During one class period, students make **oral presentations** about the nonfiction pieces they have read. This not only exposes all students to a wealth of information, it also gives students the opportunity to practice **public speaking**.

The **review lesson** pulls together all of the aspects of the unit. The teacher is given four or five choices of activities or games to use which all serve the same basic function of reviewing all of the information presented in the unit.

The **unit test** comes in two formats: all multiple choice-matching-true/false or with a mixture of matching, short answer, multiple choice, and composition. As a convenience, two different tests for each format have been included.

There are additional **support materials** included with this unit. The **extra activities** section includes suggestions for an in-class library, crossword and word search puzzles related to the novel, and extra vocabulary worksheets. There is a list of **bulletin board ideas** which gives the teacher suggestions for bulletin boards to go along with this unit. In addition, there is a list of **extra class activities** the teacher could choose from to enhance the unit or as a substitution for an exercise the teacher might feel is inappropriate for his/her class. **Answer keys** are located directly after the **reproducible student materials** throughout the unit. The student materials may be reproduced for use in the teacher's classroom without infringement of copyrights. No other portion of this unit may be reproduced without the written consent of Teacher's Pet Publications, Inc.

UNIT OBJECTIVES - *The Stranger*

1. Through reading Albert Camus' *The Stranger*, students will learn about the philosophy of existentialism.

2. Students will demonstrate their understanding of the text on four levels: factual, interpretive, critical and personal.

3. Students will study related topics such as treatment of the elderly, crime and punishment, and responsibility.

4. Students will be given the opportunity to practice reading aloud and silently to improve their skills in each area.

5. Students will answer questions to demonstrate their knowledge and understanding of the main events and characters in *The Stranger* as they relate to the author's theme development.

6. Students will enrich their vocabularies and improve their understanding of the novel through the vocabulary lessons prepared for use in conjunction with the novel.

7. The writing assignments in this unit are geared to several purposes:
    a. To have students demonstrate their abilities to inform, to persuade, or to express their own personal ideas

    > Note: Students will demonstrate ability to write effectively to <u>inform</u> by developing and organizing facts to convey information. Students will demonstrate the ability to write effectively to <u>persuade</u> by selecting and organizing relevant information, establishing an argumentative purpose, and by designing an appropriate strategy for an identified audience. Students will demonstrate the ability to write effectively to <u>express personal ideas</u> by selecting a form and its appropriate elements.

    b. To check the students' reading comprehension
    c. To make students think about the ideas presented by the novel
    d. To encourage logical thinking
    e. To provide an opportunity to practice good grammar and improve students' use of the English language.

8. Students will read aloud, report, and participate in large and small group discussions to improve their public speaking and personal interaction skills.

READING ASSIGNMENT SHEET - *The Stranger*

Date Assigned	Reading Assignment	Completion Date
	Part I: 1-3	
	Part I: 4-6	
	Part II	

UNIT OUTLINE - *The Stranger*

1 Introduction PV I:1-3	2 Read I: 1-3	3 Study ?s I:1-3 PVR I:4-6	4 Library	5 Study ?s I:4-6 PVR II
6 Study ?s II Extra Questions	7 Vocabulary	8 Writing Assignment 1	9 Nonfiction Reports	10 Group Activity
11 Reports & Discussion	12 Writing Assignment 2	13 Speaker	14 Class Activity	15 Writing Assignment 3
16 Review	17 Test			

Key: P = Preview Study Questions   V = Vocabulary Work   R = Read

STUDY GUIDE QUESTIONS

SHORT ANSWER STUDY GUIDE QUESTIONS - *The Stranger*

Part I   Chapter numbers are indicated in ( ).
1. Who is the narrator of *The Stranger*? (1)
2. What does Meursault do in the opening chapter? (1)
3. What is Meursault's reaction to his mother's death? (1)
4. Who does Meursault encounter at the beach? (2)
5. How do Meursault and Marie spend the Saturday after the funeral? (2)
6. What kind of a movie do they go see?(2)
7. Identify Emmanuel, Celeste, Raymond and Salamano. (3)
8. What does Meursault think of Salamano's relationship with his dog? (3)
9. What insights do we gain into Meursault's character judging from his interactions with Salamano and Raymond? (3)
10. What does Raymond want Meursault to do for him? (3)
11. Why do the police come to Raymond's room? (4)
12. What happens to Salamano's dog? How does Salamano react?(4)
13. Meursault tells his boss that "people never change their lives, that in any case one life is as good as another." What do we learn about Meursault from this statement? (5)
14. How does Meursault respond when Marie asks if he loves her? (5)
15. Who is Masson, and why does Meursault go to his beach house? (6)
16. How does Raymond get hurt? (6)
17. Why does Meursault return to the beach and to the rock by the water? (6)
18. What does Meursault do when he encounters the Arab at the rock? Why? (6)

Part II
1. What about Meursault upsets and frustrates his lawyer and the magistrate? (1)
2. What does the magistrate use to try to break through to Meursault's feelings of remorse or sadness? (1)
3. Why is Marie only allowed to visit Meursault one time? Does Meursault seem to care whether or not she comes back to visit? (2)
4. How does Meursault pass his time in prison? (2)
5. At Meursault's trial, why is so much made of his conduct at his mother's funeral? (3)
6. What does Celeste say concerning the murder? (3)
7. What is Marie's testimony and how does it hurt Meursault's case? (3)
8. What defense did Meursault's lawyer present? (4)
9. What was the jury's verdict? (4)
10. What does Meursault tell the chaplain? (5)
11. What does Meursault try to explain to the chaplain after he becomes angry? (6)

KEY: SHORT ANSWER STUDY GUIDE QUESTIONS - *The Stranger*

Part I   Chapter numbers are indicated in ( ).

1. Who is the narrator of *The Stranger*? (1)
    A man named Monsieur Meursault is the narrator.

2. What does Meursault do in the opening chapter? (1)
    Informed of his mother's death, Meursault goes to the home for the aged where she has lived. He sits in vigil for her overnight and attends her burial the next day.

3. What is Meursault's reaction to his mother's death? (1)
    He is emotionally unaffected by it. He goes through the motions of what is expected of him yet appears to be unconcerned. He does not weep or seem at all grieved at his mother's death.

4. Who does Meursault encounter at the beach? (2)
    He sees Marie, a girl who had once worked at the same office where he worked.

5. How do Meursault and Marie spend the Saturday after the funeral? (2)
    They swim and flirt with each other and go to the movies together. Marie spends the night with Meursault.

6. What kind of a movie do they go see?
    They see a comedy. Meursault comments that the movie "was funny in parts, but otherwise it was just too stupid." (2)

7. Identify Emmanuel, Celeste, Raymond and Salamano. (3)
    Emmanuel is a dispatcher where Meursault works. Celeste owns a restaurant where Meursault often eats. Raymond is Meursault's neighbor who claims to work as a warehouse guard, but is thought to be a pimp. Salamano is Meursault's neighbor who mistreats his dog.

8. What does Meursault think of Salamano's relationship with his dog? (3)
    He basically thinks nothing of Salamano's cruel treatment of his dog. Both Celeste and Raymond mention that it is pitiful, but Meursault just accepts it with no comment.

9. What insights do we gain into Meursault's character judging from his interactions with Salamano and Raymond? (3)
    Meursault does not judge either man. As to the dog's life being pitiful, he just thinks, "Who's to say?" He listens to Raymond because he finds Raymond to be somewhat interesting and because he has no reason to not listen to him.

10. What does Raymond want Meursault to do for him? (3)

    He wants Meursault to write a letter to his mistress so she will come back to him and he can further punish her.

11. Why do the police come to Raymond's room? (4)

    A neighbor called the police to come because Raymond is beating his mistress. Note that although Marie asks Meursault to call the police, he refuses saying simply that he does not like the police.

12. What happens to Salamano's dog? How does Salamano react?(4)

    It got away from him while they were out. Salamano is distressed; he loved the dog even though he often did not act so. He goes to Meursault to talk about his loss.

13. Meursault tells his boss that "people never change their lives, that in any case one life is as good as another." What do we learn about Meursault from this statement? (5)

    It reflects Meursault's attitude that nothing matters. One life is as good as another; there is no good or bad, no right or wrong; things just are the way they are. Whether things are one way or another makes no difference. He doesn't judge Raymond or pity Salamano's dog, care whether or not he moves to Paris, or feel grief at his mother's death. He just takes everything with an indifferent attitude.

14. How does Meursault respond when Marie asks if he loves her? (5)

    He says that it doesn't mean anything, but that he probably doesn't love her. Yet later he says he would marry her if she wanted to get married, although being married has no particular meaning or significance to him.

15. Who is Masson, and why does Meursault go to his beach house? (6)

    Masson is a friend of Raymond who invited Raymond to bring his friends to the beach house for a weekend. Raymond invited Meursault and Marie, who gladly accepted the invitation, since they love the sea and the sun.

16. How does Raymond get hurt? (6)

    While walking on the beach, he, Masson and Meursault encounter the "Arabs," we are told are the brother of Raymond's mistress and the brother's friend. During the brief fight, Raymond is cut on the arm and mouth.

17. Why does Meursault return to the beach and to the rock by the water? (6)

    He is too tired to climb the stairs to the beach house and to face the women. Since he thinks it makes no difference if he climbs the stairs or not, he decides to take the easy route and go back to the beach. As he walks, the sun becomes hotter and he heads back to the shade and cool water by the rock.

18. What does Meursault do when he encounters the Arab at the rock? Why? (6)

He shoots him. The first shot was an accident; he was dazed by the sun, couldn't see because of the sweat in his eyes, and he pulled the trigger of the gun before he realized what he had done. The other four shots he fired into the corpse remain unexplained.

Part II

1. What about Meursault upsets and frustrates his lawyer and the magistrate? (1)

Meursault's lack of emotion or remorse concerning both his crime and his mother's death cause both his lawyer and the magistrate to become angry and unsure of how to deal with him.

2. What does the magistrate use to try to break through to Meursault's feelings of remorse or sadness?

He waves a crucifix in front of Meursault and appeals to his religious beliefs. What the magistrate discovers is that Meursault truly does not believe in God or any kind of religion.

3. Why is Marie only allowed to visit Meursault one time? Does Meursault seem to care whether or not she comes back to visit? (2)

She is not allowed to visit more because she is not his wife. He doesn't seem to care very much. What he misses is their physical relationship.

4. How does Meursault pass his time in prison? (2)

He sleeps most of the time, and in the remaining hours, he tries to remember details of his room at home and does other mind games, and tends to things like meals and other events of the prison routine.

5. At Meursault's trial, why is so much made of his conduct at his mother's funeral? (3)

Meursault's lack of emotion at his own mother's funeral gives the prosecution evidence that Meursault is a hard-hearted man, a cold-blooded killer.

6. What does Celeste say concerning the murder? (3)

He tries to help Meursault, but all he can offer is that the murder was "bad luck."

7. What is Marie's testimony and how does it hurt Meursault's case? (3)

She relates the events of the day they began their relationship -- their meeting at the beach, the movie, and their night together. Since these events took place on the day after his mother's funeral, they reinforce the prosecution's idea that Meursault is without morals; he is out having a good time, living it up at a time when he should be in mourning.

8. What defense did Meursault's lawyer present? (4)

He tried to show Meursault as a hard worker, a "model son" who did what he thought was best for his mother, and a caring individual. He left out any mention of the funeral, since his actions there were indefensible.

9. What was the jury's verdict? (4)
    Meursault was found guilty and sentenced to death at the guillotine.

10. What does Meursault tell the chaplain? (5)
    He tells him that he does not believe in God and is not at all even interested in the subject. He says he has no time to spare for things that hold no interest for him.

11. What does Meursault try to explain to the chaplain after he becomes angry? (6)
    He tries to make the chaplain see that one life is as good (or bad) as another, that everyone waits for his execution, that nothing matters because ultimately there is only "nothing."

MULTIPLE CHOICE STUDY GUIDE/QUIZ QUESTIONS - *The Stranger*

Part I

1. From what point of view is the novel written?
    a. It is written from the first person point of view.
    b. It is written from the third person point of view.
    c. It is written from the third person omniscient author point of view.

2. What does Meursault do in the opening chapter?
    a. He looks for a new job.
    b. He quits school and begins to live the life of an artist.
    c. He attends his mother's funeral.
    d. He takes the train to Paris for the weekend.

3. What is Meursault's reaction to his mother's death?
    a. He screams and cries, and has to be restrained.
    b. He is crushed, but bears his grief stoically.
    c. He says he never loved her anyway, and he is glad to be rid of her.
    d. He is emotionally unaffected, and doesn't weep or grieve.

4. Who does Meursault encounter at the beach?
    a. He meets his old college roommate.
    b. He meets a girl who had once worked at the same office as he did.
    c. He meets a friend of his mother's from the nursing home.
    d. He meets his aunt, his only living relative.

5. Which of the following is not one of the ways Marie and Meursault spend the Saturday after the funeral?
    a. They swim.
    b. They flirt.
    c. They had lunch at his favorite restaurant.
    d. They spent the night together.

6. What kind of a movie did they go to see?
    a. It was a comedy.
    b. It was a musical.
    c. It was a documentary about the war.
    d. It was a cartoon from America.

The Stranger Multiple Choice Study Questions Page 2

7-10. Match each of the following characters with the correct description.

    7. Emmanuel   A. restaurant owner
    8. Celeste   B. claims to work as a warehouse guard
    9. Raymond   C. a dispatcher
    10. Salamano   D. mistreats the dog

11. What does Meursault think of his neighbor's relationship with his dog?
    a. He thinks it is cruel.
    b. He accepts it with no comment.
    c. He approves because he doesn't like animals.
    d. He pities the two of them, because they only have each other.

12. What insights do we gain into Meursault's character from his interactions with Salamano and Raymond?
    a. He is harsh and judgmental.
    b. He does not judge either man.
    c. He uses people for his own advantage.
    d. He is insane.

13. What does Raymond want Meursault to do for him?
    a. He wants Meursault to invest his money, because Meursault does well with stocks.
    b. He wants Meursault to move in with him and share an apartment.
    c. He wants Meursault to write a letter to his (Raymond's) mistress so she will come back to him.
    d. He wants Meursault to take a vacation cruise with him.

14. True or False: The police have been called to Raymond's room because he is beating his mistress.
    a. True
    b. False

15. True or False: Meursault makes the call because Marie has asked him to.
    a. True
    b. False

16. What happens to Salamano's dog?
    a. It gets away from him while they are out.
    b. The dogcatchers take it because it is sick.
    c. It is run over by a delivery truck.
    d. It drops dead of old age.

The Stranger Multiple Choice Study Questions Page 3

17. True or False: Salamano is glad to be rid of the dog.
    a. True
    b. False

18. Meursault tells his boss that "people never change their lives, that in any case one life is as good as another." What do we learn about Meursault from this statement?
    a. He is a philosopher.
    b. He takes everything with an indifferent attitude.
    c. He is not respectful to his superiors.
    d. He values life above all else.

19. How does Meursault respond when Marie asks if he loves her?
    a. He says it doesn't mean anything, but he probably doesn't love her.
    b. He says he loves her very much.
    c. He changes the subject.
    d. He tells her he loves her even though he doesn't, just because it's easier than telling the truth.

20. True or False: Meursault also tells Marie that no matter how he feels, he would never marry her because he never wants to get married.
    a. True
    b. False

21. Who is Masson?
    a. He is the owner of a vineyard where Meursault wants to work.
    b. He is Meursault's boss.
    c. He is a friend of Raymond.
    d. He is Marie's former lover who has returned for her.

22. Why does Meursault go to the beach house?
    a. He wants to get away from Marie.
    b. He has been invited by Raymond.
    c. He has been evicted from his apartment and has nowhere else to go.
    d. He is thinking of buying it for an investment.

23. How does Raymond get hurt?
    a. He and his companions encounter the "Arabs" and he is cut by one man's knife.
    b. He is diving off a rock into the ocean and slips.
    c. He is attacked by a school of jellyfish.
    d. He is running in his bare feet and cuts his foot on a sharp piece of clam shell.

The Stranger Multiple Choice Study Questions Page 4

24. True or False: Meursault takes the easy route and goes back to the beach.
    a. True
    b. False

25. What does Meursault do when he encounters the man at the rock?
    a. He shoots him.
    b. He knifes him.
    c. He starts a fist fight.
    d. He strangles the man.

26. Are his actions after his initial reaction explained?
    a. Yes, they are.
    b. No, they are not.

The Stranger Multiple Choice Study Questions Page 5

Part II

27. True or False: Meursault's lack of emotion or remorse concerning his crime and his mother's death cause both his lawyer and the magistrate to become angry and unsure of how to deal with him.
    a. True
    b. False

28. What does the magistrate use to try to break through to Meursault feelings?
    a. He uses a picture of Meursault's mother to remind him of his loss.
    b. He uses hypnosis.
    c. He waves a crucifix and appeals to his religious beliefs.
    d. He orders that Meursault be kept in solitary confinement until he repents.

29. Why is Marie allowed only one visit to Meursault?
    a. The guards are afraid she will smuggle in poison so he can kill himself.
    b. It is too expensive. Visitors must bribe the guards to get in, and she can only afford one bribe.
    c. She is not his wife.
    d. She has been arrested as an accomplice to the crime and is in jail herself.

30. Does Meursault seem to care whether or not she comes back to visit?
    a. Yes, he does.
    b. No, he doesn't.

31. Which of the following is not one of the things Meursault does to pass the time in prison?
    a. He sleeps most of the time.
    b. He tries to remember details of his room at home.
    c. He reads and studies in the prison library.
    d. He tends to meals and other events of the prison routine.

32. True or False: At Meursault's trial, the prosecutor uses Meursault's lack of emotion at his mother's funeral as evidence that Meursault is a hard-hearted man and a cold-blooded killer.
    a. True
    b. False

33. What does Celeste say concerning the murder?
    a. He says that he always thought Meursault had a violent streak.
    b. He said he was sure it was self-defense.
    c. He said it was bad luck.
    d. He said the Arab got what he deserved.

The Stranger Multiple Choice Study Questions Page 6

34. What is Marie's testimony?
    a. She tells about the day of the murder.
    b. She tells about Raymond's mistreatment of his mistress.
    c. She tells about Meursault's childhood.
    d. She tells about the events of the day she met Meursault.

35. Does Marie's testimony help or hurt Meursault?
    a. It helps.
    b. It hurts.

36. True or False: Meursault's lawyer tried to show that Meursault was temporarily insane because he was grieving over his mother's death.
    a. True
    b. False

37. What was the jury's verdict?
    a. They found Meursault guilty and he was sentenced to death at the guillotine.
    b. They found Meursault not guilty by reason of insanity and sent him to an asylum.
    c. They found Meursault guilty with mitigating circumstances and sentenced him to life in prison.
    d. They found that Meursault acted in self- defense and he was released.

38. What does Meursault tell the chaplain?
    a. He says he has had a conversion and asks to be baptized.
    b. He says he does not believe in God and has no time for things that do not interest him.
    c. He is sorry for all he has done and asks for forgiveness.
    d. He wishes he could go back and do it all over again; he would do things differently.

39. What does Meursault do after the chaplain responds to his statement?
    a. He tries to make the chaplain see that nothing matters because ultimately there is only nothing.
    b. He kneels down and starts praying, and asks to be forgiven.
    c. He finally breaks down and laughs hysterically.
    d. He called for the guards and asked to have the chaplain removed.

ANSWER KEY - MULTIPLE CHOICE STUDY/QUIZ QUESTIONS
The Stranger

Part I	Part II
1. A	27. A
2. C	28. C
3. D	29. C
4. B	30. B
5. C	31. C
6. A	32. A
7. C	33. C
8. A	34. D
9. B	35. B
10. D	36. B
11. B	37. A
12. B	38. B
13. C	39. A
14. A	
15. B	
16. A	
17. B	
18. B	
19. A	
20. B	
21. C	
22. B	
23. A	
24. A	
25. A	
26. B	

PREREADING VOCABULARY WORKSHEETS

VOCABULARY - *The Stranger*

Part I Chapters 1-3 Part I: Using Prior Knowledge and Contextual Clues
Below are the sentences in which the vocabulary words appear in the text. Read the sentence. Use any clues you can find in the sentence combined with your prior knowledge, and write what you think the underlined words mean on the lines provided.

1. He's the one who should have offered his <u>condolences</u>.

2. While not an <u>atheist</u>, Maman had never in her life given a thought to religion.

3. In the little mortuary he told me that he'd come to the home because he was <u>destitute</u>.

4. He kept hacking into a large checkered handkerchief, and every cough was like a <u>convulsion</u>.

5. The uncomfortable <u>vigil</u> had left their faces ashen looking.

6. The men moved toward the casket with a <u>pall</u>.

7. Strange, floppy, thick-rimmed ears stuck out through his fine, white hair, and I was struck by their blood-red color next to the <u>pallor</u> of his face.

8. ... more people, voices, the village, waiting in front of a cafe, the <u>incessant</u> drone of the motor, and my joy when the bus entered the nest of lights that was Algiers. . . . .

9. The <u>matinees</u> had all started, I guess.

10. Soon afterwards, with the streetcars running less often and the sky already blue above the trees and the lamps, the neighborhood emptied out, almost <u>imperceptibly</u>, until the first cat slowly made its way across the now deserted street.

Vocabulary - *The Stranger* Part I Chapters 1-3 Continued

Part II: Determining the Meaning

Match the vocabulary words to their dictionary definitions. If there are words for which you cannot figure out the definition by contextual clues and by process of elimination, look them up in a dictionary.

___ 1. condolences
___ 2. atheist
___ 3. destitute
___ 4. convulsion
___ 5. vigil
___ 6. pall

___ 7. pallor
___ 8. incessant
___ 9. matinees
___ 10. imperceptibly

A. ceaseless; continual
B. lacking the means of subsistence; left friendless
C. a period of watchful attention; a watch kept by night
D. expressions of sympathy
E. very slight, gradual or subtle
F. violent and involuntary spasmodic contraction of the muscles; commotion
G. one who disbelieves the existence of a God
H. entertainments held in the afternoon
I. unnatural paleness, as from fear, ill health or death
J. cloth covering a coffin; a square, linen-covered piece of cardboard used to cover a chalice; something that overspreads with darkness and gloom

Vocabulary - *The Stranger* Part I Chapters 4-6

Part I: Using Prior Knowledge and Contextual Clues
Below are the sentences in which the vocabulary words appear in the text. Read the sentence. Use any clues you can find in the sentence combined with your prior knowledge, and write what you think the underlined words mean on the lines provided.

11. The look on Raymond's face changed, but he didn't say anything for a minute, and then he asked, in a meek voice, if he could pick up his cigarette.

12. He was looking all over the place, turning around, peering into the darkness of the entryway, muttering incoherently, and then he started searching the street again with his little red eyes.

13. And from the peculiar little noise coming through the partition, I realized he was crying.

14. He told me he wanted to talk to me about a plan of his that was still pretty vague.

15. Then I told her about my boss's proposition and she said she'd love to see Paris.

16. I had already finished and she was still checking away with the same zeal.

17. For the first time since I'd known him, and with a furtive gesture, he offered me his hand, and I felt the scales on his skin.

18. I found it a little repulsive.

19. Before we reached the edge of the plateau, we could already see the motionless sea and, farther out, a massive, drowsy-looking promontory in the clear water.

20. But most of the time, he was just a form shimmering before my eyes in the fiery air.

Vocabulary - *The Stranger* Part I Chapters 4-6 Continued

Part II: Determining the Meaning

Match the vocabulary words to their dictionary definitions. If there are words for which you cannot figure out the definition by contextual clues and by process of elimination, look them up in a dictionary.

___ 11. meek
___ 12. incoherently
___ 13. peculiar
___ 14. vague
___ 15. proposition
___ 16. zeal
___ 17. furtive
___ 18. repulsive
___ 19. promontory
___ 20. fiery

A. putting forth a plan, idea, or scheme for consideration
B. unduly patient or submissive; gentle; mild; kind
C. intensely hot as winds or desert sands; passionate
D. in a manner wishing to escape observation; secret
E. a high point of land or rock projecting into the sea
F. causing repugnance or aversion; tending to drive back
G. without logical connection; rambling; uncoordinated
H. indefinite; indistinct
I. passionate ardor in behalf of a person, cause or object
J. strange; odd; uncommon; unusual

Vocabulary - *The Stranger* Part II Chapters 1-3

Part I: Using Prior Knowledge and Contextual Clues

Below are the sentences in which the vocabulary words appear in the text. Read the sentence. Use any clues you can find in the sentence combined with your prior knowledge, and write what you think the underlined words mean on the lines provided.

21. I pointed out to him that none of this had anything to do with my case, but all he said was that it was obvious I had never had any dealings with the law.

22. He took out a silver crucifix which he brandished as he came toward me.

23. ... and asking me if I believed in God. I said no. He sat down indignantly.

24. The result was that our discussions became more cordial.

25. Then very quickly and still in a very loud voice she said yes, that I would be acquitted and that we would go swimming again.

26. The only oasis of silence was next to me where the small young man and the old woman were gazing at each other.

27. Right after you, there's a parricide coming up.

28. Flipping through a file, the prosecutor asked her bluntly when our "liaison" had begun.

29. He wanted to know if it was just by chance that I hadn't intervened when Raymond had beaten up his girlfriend, ...

30. They had before them the basest of crimes, a crime made worse than sordid by the fact that they were dealing with a monster, a man without morals.

Vocabulary - *The Stranger* Part II Chapters 1-3 Continued

Part II: Determining the Meaning

Match the vocabulary words to their dictionary definitions. If there are words for which you cannot figure out the definition by contextual clues and by process of elimination, look them up in a dictionary.

___ 21. obvious
___ 22. brandished
___ 23. indignantly
___ 24. cordial
___ 25. acquitted
___ 26. oasis
___ 27. parricide
___ 28. liaison
___ 29. intervened
___ 30. sordid

A. warmly friendly; stimulating; a liqueur
B. any place or part of one's experience that is refreshingly different; a fertile spot in the desert
C. manifest; evident; exposed
D. dirty; squalid; morally mean or base
E. righteously angry; displeasure at something deemed unworthy
F. interfered; came between
G. flourished; waved or shook a weapon
H. pronounced not guilty; discharged of obligation or debt
I. crime of killing one's father or either parent or anyone to whom reverence is owed
J. an illicit intimacy between a man and woman; a cooperative relationship maintained to ensure concerted action

Vocabulary - *The Stranger* Part II Chapters 4-5

Part I: Using Prior Knowledge and Contextual Clues

Below are the sentences in which the vocabulary words appear in the text. Read the sentence. Use any clues you can find in the sentence combined with your prior knowledge, and write what you think the underlined words mean on the lines provided.

31. Only bits and pieces---a gesture or a long but isolated tirade--- caught my attention or aroused my interest.

32. The gist of what he was saying, if I understood him correctly, was that my crime was premeditated.

33. What he was saying was plausible.

34. Not once during the preliminary hearings did this man show emotion over his heinous offense."

35. According to him, the imagination recoiled before such an odious offense.

36. But all the long speeches, all the interminable days and hours that people had spent talking about my soul, had left me with the impression of a colorless swirling river that was making me dizzy.

37. What really counted was the possibility of escape, a leap to freedom, out of the implacable ritual, a wild run for it that would give whatever chance for hope there was.

38. They were slender and sinewy and they reminded me of two nimble animals.

39. Even there, in that kind of home where lives were fading out, evening was a kind of wistful respite.

40. For everything to be consummated, for me to feel less alone, I had only to wish that there be a large crowd of spectators the day of my execution and that they greet me with cries of hate.

Vocabulary - *The Stranger* - Part II Chapters 4-5 Continued

Part II: Determining the Meaning

Match the vocabulary words to their dictionary definitions. If there are words for which you cannot figure out the definition by contextual clues and by process of elimination, look them up in a dictionary.

___ 31. tirade   A. detestable; highly offensive
___ 32. premeditated   B. full of tendons; tough; stringy
___ 33. plausible   C. culminated; completed; fulfilled
___ 34. heinous   D. appearance of truth or reason; seeming worthy of acceptance
___ 35. odious   E. long outburst of denunciation; a vehement speech
___ 36. interminable   F. temporary relief
___ 37. implacable   G. planned beforehand
___ 38. sinewy   H. cannot be appeased or pacified
___ 39. respite   I. hateful; wicked or criminal; atrocious
___ 40. consummated   J. unending; endless, or seemingly so

ANSWER KEY - VOCABULARY
The Stranger

Part I Chapters 1-3

1. D
2. G
3. B
4. F
5. C
6. J
7. I
8. A
9. H
10. E

Part I Chapters 4- 6

11. B
12. G
13. J
14. H
15. A
16. I
17. D
18. F
19. E
20. C

Part II Chapters 1- 3

21. C
22. G
23. E
24. A
25. H
26. B
27. I
28. J
29. F
30. D

Part II Chapters 4 -5

31. E
32. G
33. D
34. I
35. A
36. J
37. H
38. B
39. F
40. C

DAILY LESSONS

LESSON ONE

Objectives
    1. To introduce *The Stranger* unit.
    2. To distribute books and other related materials
    3. To preview the study questions for Part I:1-3
    4. To familiarize students with the vocabulary for Part I:1-3

Activity #1
Write the following poem by Stephen Crane on the board:
    A man said to the universe:
    "Sir, I exist!"
    "However," replied the universe,
    "The fact has not created in me
    A sense of obligation."
Use this poem as a springboard for a discussion about what it is that gives meaning to our lives.

Activity #2
Write the following definition (from the American Heritage Dictionary) on the board:
    existentialism - A body of ethical thought, current in the 19th and 20th centuries, centering about the uniqueness and isolation of individual experience in a universe indifferent or even hostile to man, regarding human existence as unexplainable, and emphasizing man's freedom of choice and responsibility for the consequences of his acts.

Talk about the definition, examining each part and putting in simpler terms what each part means. Introduce Albert Camus, giving students some biographical information about this author. Explain that the book students are about to read, *The Stranger*, by Albert Camus has many qualities of existentialism in it. Tell students to write down the definition of existentialism and to keep it in mind as they read the book.

Activity #3
Distribute the materials students will use in this unit. Explain in detail how students are to use these materials.

Study Guides Students should read the study guide questions for each reading assignment prior to beginning the reading assignment to get a feeling for what events and ideas are important in the section they are about to read. After reading the section, students will (as a class or individually) answer the questions to review the important events and ideas from that section of the book. Students should keep the study guides as study materials for the unit test.

Vocabulary   Prior to reading a reading assignment, students will do vocabulary work related to the section of the book they are about to read. Following the completion of the reading of the book, there will be a vocabulary review of all the words used in the vocabulary assignments. Students should keep their vocabulary work as study materials for the unit test.

Reading Assignment Sheet   You need to fill in the reading assignment sheet to let students know by when their reading has to be completed. You can either write the assignment sheet up on a side blackboard or bulletin board and leave it there for students to see each day, or you can "ditto" copies for each student to have. In either case, you should advise students to become very familiar with the reading assignments so they know what is expected of them.

Extra Activities Center   The Unit Resource portion of this unit contains suggestions for an extra library of related books and articles in your classroom as well as crossword and word search puzzles. Make an extra activities center in your room where you will keep these materials for students to use. (Bring the books and articles in from the library and keep several copies of the puzzles on hand.) Explain to students that these materials are available for students to use when they finish reading assignments or other class work early.

Nonfiction Assignment Sheet   Explain to students that they each are to read at least one non-fiction piece from the in-class library at some time during the unit. Students will fill out a nonfiction assignment sheet after completing the reading to help you evaluate their reading experiences and to help the students think about and evaluate their own reading experiences.

Books   Each school has its own rules and regulations regarding student use of school books. Advise students of the procedures that are normal for your school.

Activity #3
Show students how to preview the study questions and do the prereading vocabulary work for Part I:1-3 of *The Stranger*. If students do not finish this assignment during this class period, they should complete it prior to the next class meeting.

NONFICTION ASSIGNMENT SHEET
(To be completed after reading the required nonfiction article)

Name _____ Date _____

Title of Nonfiction Read _____

Written By _____ Publication Date _____

I. Factual Summary: Write a short summary of the piece you read.

II. Vocabulary
 1. With which vocabulary words in the piece did you encounter some degree of difficulty?

 2. How did you resolve your lack of understanding with these words?

III. Interpretation: What was the main point the author wanted you to get from reading his work?

IV. Criticism
 1. With which points of the piece did you agree or find easy to accept? Why?

 2. With which points of the piece did you disagree or find difficult to believe? Why?

V. Personal Response: What do you think about this piece? OR How does this piece influence your ideas?

LESSON TWO

Objectives
1. To read Part I:1-3
2. To give students practice reading orally
3. To evaluate students' oral reading

Activity

Have students read Part I:1-3 of *The Stranger* out loud in class. You probably know the best way to get readers with your class; pick students at random, ask for volunteers, or use whatever method works best for your group. If you have not yet completed an oral reading evaluation for your students this marking period, this would be a good opportunity to do so. A form is included with this unit for your convenience.

If students do not complete reading Part I:1-3 in class, they should do so prior to your next class meeting.

LESSON THREE

Objectives
1. To review the main events and ideas from Part I:1-3
2. To preview the study questions for Part I:4-6
3. To familiarize students with the vocabulary in Part I:4-6
4. To read Part I:4-6

Activity #1
Give students a few minutes to formulate answers for the study guide questions for Part I:1-3, and then discuss the answers to the questions in detail. Write the answers on the board or overhead transparency so students can have the correct answers for study purposes. Note: It is a good practice in public speaking and leadership skills for individual students to take charge of leading the discussions of the study questions. Perhaps a different student could go to the front of the class and lead the discussion each day that the study questions are discussed during this unit. Of course, the teacher should guide the discussion when appropriate and be sure to fill in any gaps the students leave.

Activity #2
Give students about fifteen minutes to preview the study questions for Part I:4-6 of *The Stranger* and to do the related vocabulary work.

Activity #3
Tell students to read Part I:4-6 of *The Stranger* prior to your next class period. If there is time remaining in this period, students may begin reading silently.

ORAL READING EVALUATION

Name _____ Class_____ Date _____

SKILL	EXCELLENT	GOOD	AVERAGE	FAIR	POOR
Fluency	5	4	3	2	1
Clarity	5	4	3	2	1
Audibility	5	4	3	2	1
Pronunciation	5	4	3	2	1
_____	5	4	3	2	1
_____	5	4	3	2	1

Total _____   Grade _____

Comments:

LESSON FOUR

Objectives

    1. To give students the opportunity to explore nonfiction topics related to the story
    2. To give students the opportunity to use the library
    3. To broaden students' knowledge of our world
    4. To hold writing conferences with individual students

Activity #1

Take students to the library. Explain to them that this is their opportunity to complete the nonfiction reading assignment which accompanies this unit. Students are to find nonfiction books or articles in some way relating to *The Stranger*. Students are to use this time to find nonfiction materials that interest them and to begin reading. Remind students to complete the Nonfiction Assignment Sheet after they have done their reading.

Remind students that they will be giving a little oral report about their nonfiction reading in Lesson Nine. (Give students a day and a date.)

Suggested Topics (Feel free to add to this list.)
    Care of the elderly
    Nursing homes
    Death penalty cases
    Existentialism
    Philosophy
    Crime and punishment
    Jury duty
    Criminal psychology
    Articles of criticism about *The Stranger*
    Biographical information about Camus (and others who were influenced by existentialism)
    Ways to cope with death and grief
    Family relationships
    How to be involved in successful relationships

LESSON FIVE

Objectives
    1. To review the main ideas and events from Part I:4-6
    2. To preview and read Part II

Activity #1

Give students a few minutes to formulate answers to the study questions for Part I:4-6. Discuss students' answers and write the "correct" answers on the board for students to copy for study use.

Activity #2

Tell students that prior to your next class meeting they should do the prereading and reading work for Part II of the book. They may use this class period to work on this assignment.

LESSON SIX

Objectives
1. To review the main ideas of Part II
2. To discuss *The Stranger* on interpretive and critical levels

Activity #1
Take a few minutes at the beginning of the period to review the study questions for Part II.

Activity #2
Choose the questions from the Extra Discussion Questions/Writing Assignments which seem most appropriate for your students. A class discussion of these questions is most effective if students have been given the opportunity to formulate answers to the questions prior to the discussion. To this end, you may either have all the students formulate answers to all the questions, divide your class into groups and assign one or more questions to each group, or you could assign one question to each student in your class. The option you choose will make a difference in the amount of class time needed for this activity.

Activity #3
After students have had ample time to formulate answers to the questions, begin your class discussion of the questions and the ideas presented by the questions. Be sure students take notes during the discussion so they have information to study for the unit test.

LESSON SEVEN

Objective
To review all of the vocabulary work done in this unit

Activity
Choose one (or more) of the vocabulary review activities listed below and spend your class period as directed in the activity. Some of the materials for these review activities are located in the Vocabulary Resource section of this unit.

EXTRA WRITING ASSIGNMENTS/DISCUSSION QUESTIONS - *The Stranger*

<u>Interpretation</u>
1. What point of view does Camus use for *The Stranger*? How does this contribute to our understanding of the themes in the story?
2. Write a list of the main events in *The Stranger*.
3. Is the story of *The Stranger* believable? Why or why not?
4. Where is the climax of the story?
5. Are the characters in *The Stranger* stereotypes? If so, why are stereotypes used? If not, explain how they merit individuality?
6. What are the main conflicts in the story, and how are they resolved?
7. Why was the novel divided into two parts? What are the characteristics of each part?

<u>Critical</u>
8. Is Meursault's death in the book inevitable? Of course everyone dies, but why didn't Camus write the story with a happy ending--with Marie and Meursault living happily ever after?
9. Are Meursault's actions believably motivated? Explain why or why not.
10. What is the role of the Marie in the story? Why was she included?
11. Characterize Albert Camus' style of writing. How does it contribute to the value of the novel?
12. Compare and contrast Meursault and Raymond.
13. Who was responsible for the death of the Arab? Explain your choice.
14. What function does the character of the woman at the restaurant serve in the novel?
15. What characteristics of existentialism are present in the novel, and how is each shown?
16. Compare and contrast the magistrate and the chaplain (priest).
17. People seem to go to Meursault for advice or to ask his opinions. Why?
18. Is Meursault as uncaring as he seems to be?
19. Why did Meursault not jump at the chance to go to Paris?
20. How was Meursault different from his usual self on the day of the murder?
21. Why did Meursault want a crowd of people at his execution?
22. Explain the significance of the title *The Stranger*.

<u>Personal Response</u>
23. If this story were told in the first person narrative by Marie, how would the story and its effect have changed?
24. Who is responsible for Meursault's situation? Explain why.
25. *The Stranger* is a short novel. Could anything have been gained by including more scenes from the time before or after the events of the story? If so, what could have been added and for what purpose. If not, explain why not.
26. Did you enjoy reading *The Stranger*? Why or why not?
27. Would you have been Meursault's friend? Why or why not?

VOCABULARY REVIEW ACTIVITIES

1. Divide your class into two teams and have an old-fashioned spelling or definition bee.

2. Give each of your students (or students in groups of two, three or four) a *The Stranger* Vocabulary Word Search Puzzle. The person (group) to find all of the vocabulary words in the puzzle first wins.

3. Give students a *The Stranger* Vocabulary Word Search Puzzle without the word list. The person or group to find the most vocabulary words in the puzzle wins.

4. Use a *The Stranger* Vocabulary Crossword Puzzle. Put the puzzle onto a transparency on the overhead projector (so everyone can see it), and do the puzzle together as a class.

5. Give students a *The Stranger* Vocabulary Matching Worksheet to do.

6. Divide your class into two teams. Use *The Stranger* vocabulary words with their letters jumbled as a word list. Student 1 from Team A faces off against Student 1 from Team B. You write the first jumbled word on the board. The first student (1A or 1B) to unscramble the word wins the chance for his/her team to score points. If 1A wins the jumble, go to student 2A and give him/her a definition. He/she must give you the correct spelling of the vocabulary word which fits that definition. If he/she does, Team A scores a point, and you give student 3A a definition for which you expect a correctly spelled matching vocabulary word. Continue giving Team A definitions until some team member makes an incorrect response. An incorrect response sends the game back to the jumbled-word face off, this time with students 2A and 2B. Instead of repeating giving definitions to the first few students of each team, continue with the student after the one who gave the last incorrect response on the team. For example, if Team B wins the jumbled-word face-off, and student 5B gave the last incorrect answer for Team B, you would start this round of definition questions with student 6B, and so on. The team with the most points wins!

7. Have students write a story in which they correctly use as many vocabulary words as possible. Have students read their compositions orally! Post the most original compositions on your bulletin board!

LESSON EIGHT

<u>Objectives</u>
1. To give students the opportunity to practice writing to inform
2. To give the teacher the opportunity to evaluate students' writing skills
3. To help students prepare for their oral presentations

<u>Activity</u>
Distribute Writing Assignment #1. Discuss the directions in detail and then give students ample time to complete the assignment.

LESSON NINE

<u>Objectives</u>
1. To widen the breadth of students' knowledge about the topics discussed or touched upon in *The Stranger*
2. To check students' nonfiction reading assignments

<u>Activity</u>
Ask each student to give a brief oral report about the nonfiction work he/she read for the nonfiction reading assignment. Your criteria for evaluating this report will vary depending on the level of your students. You may wish for students to give a complete report without using notes of any kind, or you may want students to read directly from a written report, or you may want to do something in between these two extremes. Just make students aware of your criteria in ample time for them to prepare their reports.

Start with one student's report. After that, ask if anyone else in the class has read about a topic related to the first student's report. If no one has, choose another student at random. After each report, be sure to ask if anyone has a report related to the one just completed. That will help keep a continuity during the discussion of the reports.

WRITING ASSIGNMENT #1 - *The Stranger*

PROMPT

You have read at least one article of nonfiction relating to *The Stranger*. Now you are to write a composition in which you summarize your article(s). This is to help you review the information as well as to help prepare you for your oral presentation.

PREWRITING

Your reading has been done, and you probably have some notes on paper sitting in front of you. Look at your notes and begin to organize them. Arrange the notes in an order that makes sense: chronological order (order of time that the events happen) is often appropriate.

DRAFTING

Start with a paragraph in which you introduce your topic. In the body of your paper write your summary. Finally, write a paragraph in which you give your opinions about your topic (tell whether you agree or disagree with the article, for example).

PROMPT

When you finish the rough draft of your paper, ask a student who sits near you to read it. After reading your rough draft, he/she should tell you what he/she liked best about your work, which parts were difficult to understand, and ways in which your work could be improved. Reread your paper considering your critic's comments, and make the corrections you think are necessary.

PROOFREADING

Do a final proofreading of your paper double-checking your grammar, spelling, organization, and the clarity of your ideas.

LESSON TEN AND ELEVEN

Objectives
1. To study the novel more closely through all six chapters.
2. To give students the opportunity to practice their personal interaction skills in a small group setting.
3. To give students the opportunity to practice their public speaking skills as they report their small group findings.

Activity #1

Divide the class into six groups. Each group should be assigned one of the following topics: blame/fault/guilt, colors, images (sea, sun, sleep, things being unclear in M's mind, etc.), changes in Meursault, religion, and truth. Students within the group will each take specific chapters of *The Stranger* and find all the references to their group's topic in that chapter. Students should jot down their findings. When the individuals are done with their research, group members should get together to discuss their findings. Based on their research, they should try to draw some conclusions about the topic.

Activity #2

The groups will each report their findings and conclusions to the whole class. Each student will give his findings, and one group member will give the group's conclusions.
The teacher or a student should write down on the board or overhead all of the findings and conclusions. If you have enough room, a chart format would be helpful for students' study purposes. (Students should all take notes from the board for later study.)

LESSON TWELVE

Objectives
1. To review the material facts of the story and evaluate them
2. To give students the opportunity to practice writing to persuade
3. To give the teacher the opportunity to evaluate students' writing skills and understanding of the novel

Activity

Distribute Writing Assignment #2. Discuss the directions in detail and give students ample time to complete the assignment.

WRITING ASSIGNMENT #2 - *The Stranger*

PROMPT

One of the first things that one notices upon studying our criminal justice system is that there is a difference between "justice" and "law." One of our rights as citizens of the United States is the right to a fair trial under the law. Certain procedures have been developed to insure that one gets a fair trial. You have probably heard of someone "getting off on a technicality," which means usually that some legal procedure was not followed correctly and therefore the case against the defendant was dismissed (whether he/she was guilty or not). If you are the defendant, you celebrate. If you are the victim, you may be angry or astonished that "justice" was not served. The person who did this thing to you just waltzed out of the courtroom without punishment. Thus, you can see the difference between "justice" and "law."

Your assignment is to write a composition in which you persuade me that justice was (or was not) served in Meursault's case.

PREWRITING

Review the passages in the text relating to Meursault's trial; specifically the statements made to the court by the two attorneys. Take two pieces of scratch paper. Label one Defense and the other Prosecution. On the Defense paper, jot down the arguments Meursault's attorney made on his behalf. On the Prosecution paper, jot down the arguments the state's attorney made against Meursault. Consider the arguments on both sides. Decide whether or not the sentence the judge gave Meursault was "just" or not.

Jot down three reasons why you think the sentence was (or was not) just. Next to each reason jot down some examples, ideas or explanations to support your reason.

DRAFTING

Write a paragraph in which you introduce the idea that the sentence handed down to Meursault from the judge was (or was not) just.

Write one paragraph for each of the reasons you listed for your decision. Each paragraph should have a topic sentence stating your reason and should be filled out with examples, ideas or explanations to support your reasons.

Write one paragraph in which you draw your conclusions and bring your composition to a close.

PROOFREADING

When you finish the rough draft of your paper, ask a student who sits near you to read it. After reading your rough draft, he/she should tell you what he/she liked best about your work, which parts were difficult to understand, and ways in which your work could be improved. Reread your paper considering your critic's comments, and make the corrections you think are necessary. Do a final proofreading of your paper double-checking your grammar, spelling, organization, and the clarity of your ideas.

LESSON THIRTEEN

Objectives
1. To look at the story from a different perspective--as jurors at the trial
2. To educate students about one of their civic responsibilities--jury duty

Activity
Have a retired judge or a lawyer come to your classroom to discuss our civic responsibility of jury duty. He/she should explain to students how one is chosen for jury duty and what is expected of jurors. Many areas have a video tape that is shown to jury panels as they begin their duty. Perhaps you could borrow a copy and show it.

Follow-up: After the presentation, ask students to pretend they were jurors at Meursault's trial. Give them a few minutes to make up their minds as to whether they would have found him guilty or innocent, and then ask for a show of hands to see what the vote would have been from your student jury panel.

LESSONS FOURTEEN AND FIFTEEN

Objectives
1. To discuss the whole issue of responsibility
2. To get students to evaluate how responsibly they behave
3. To give the teacher the opportunity to evaluate students' writing skills
4. To give students the opportunity to practice writing personal opinions

Activity #1
Ask students to each write a definition for the word "responsible." After students have written their definitions, collect them and read them to the class (without identifying the writer of each definition). Tell students to consider all the aspects of responsibility that were put forth in the definitions you just read, and then work together as a class to come up with the best definition possible. Have students brainstorm a list of different kinds of responsibilities they each have. After students have completed this task, ask for students to volunteer to read their own lists. Using these lists as springboards, have the class come up with a list of responsibilities we all have (civic, personal, ethical/moral, etc.). Ask students,"How well did Meursault handle his responsibilities?" and use this as a springboard to discuss this aspect of the story. (This also acts as a transition to the next writing assignment.)

Activity #2
Distribute Writing Assignment #3. Discuss the directions in detail and give students ample time to complete the assignment. While students are working on this assignment, call individual students to your desk or some other private area for writing conferences based on the first (two) writing assignments. An evaluation form is included in this unit for your convenience.

WRITING ASSIGNMENT #3 - *The Stranger*

PROMPT

We have discussed what it means to be responsible, and you have evaluated Meursault in terms of how well he handled his responsibilities. Now it is time to turn from fiction to real life and evaluate yourself in terms of how well you handle your responsibilities. Your assignment is to answer the question, "Are you a responsible person?"

PREWRITING

You have already given some thought to what your responsibilities are. If you still have the list you brainstormed the other day in class, get it out and review it. If not, make a new list so you can see your responsibilities in a tangible, concrete way. Go down the list of responsibilities and evaluate how well you do each item. For example, if one of your responsibilities is to care for a family pet, grade yourself as to how well you carry out that responsibility. Does your parent have to constantly nag you to feed it, bathe it, take it for a walk, clean it's living space, etc., or do you do the related chores consistently without being reminded?

After you have evaluated yourself on each of the responsibilities on your list, look over your evaluations. Did you do pretty well, or have you been a little remiss in your duties? Give yourself an overall evaluation: are you very responsible, pretty responsible, somewhat responsible, not very responsible, or totally irresponsible?

DRAFTING

Write an introductory paragraph in which you introduce the main idea for your composition, that you are a very responsible, pretty responsible, somewhat responsible, not very responsible, or totally irresponsible person.

Write one paragraph for each of your responsibilities, explaining what the responsibility is and how well you handle it.

Write a paragraph in which you explain why you take responsibilities seriously (if you do) or explain why you don't take responsibilities seriously (if you don't).

PROMPT

When you finish the rough draft of your composition, ask a student who sits near you to read it. After reading your rough draft, he/she should tell you what he/she liked best about your work, which parts were difficult to understand, and ways in which your work could be improved. Reread your paper considering your critic's comments, and make the corrections you think are necessary.

PROOFREADING

Do a final proofreading of your paper double-checking your grammar, spelling, organization, and the clarity of your ideas.

WRITING EVALUATION FORM - *The Stranger*

Name _____ Date _____

      Grade _____

Grammar: excellent   good fair   poor

Spelling: excellent   good fair   poor

Punctuation: excellent   good fair   poor

Legibility: excellent   good fair poor

Strengths:

Weaknesses:

Comments/Suggestions:

LESSON SIXTEEN

Objective
    To review the main ideas presented in *The Stranger*

Activity #1
    Choose one of the review games/activities included in this unit and spend your class period as outlined there. Some materials for these activities are located in the Extra Activities section of this unit.

Activity #2
    Remind students that the Unit Test will be in the next class meeting. Stress the review of the Study Guides and their class notes as a last minute, brush-up review for homework.

REVIEW GAMES/ACTIVITIES - *The Stranger*

1. Ask the class to make up a unit test for *The Stranger*. The test should have 4 sections: matching, true/false, short answer, and essay. Students may use 1/2 period to make the test and then swap papers and use the other 1/2 class period to take a test a classmate has devised. (open book) You may want to use the unit test included in this unit or take questions from the students' unit tests to formulate your own test.

2. Take 1/2 period for students to make up true and false questions (including the answers). Collect the papers and divide the class into two teams. Draw a big tic-tac-toe board on the chalk board. Make one team X and one team O. Ask questions to each side, giving each student one turn. If the question is answered correctly, that students' team's letter (X or O) is placed in the box. If the answer is incorrect, no mark is placed in the box. The object is to get three marks in a row like tic-tac-toe. You may want to keep track of the number of games won for each team.

3. Take 1/2 period for students to make up questions (true/false and short answer). Collect the questions. Divide the class into two teams. You'll alternate asking questions to individual members of teams A & B (like in a spelling bee). The question keeps going from A to B until it is correctly answered, then a new question is asked. A correct answer does not allow the team to get another question. Correct answers are +2 points; incorrect answers are -1 point.

4. Have students pair up and quiz each other from their study guides and class notes.

5. Give students a *The Stranger* crossword puzzle to complete.

6. Divide your class into two teams. Use *The Stranger* crossword words with their letters jumbled as a word list. Student 1 from Team A faces off against Student 1 from Team B. You write the first jumbled word on the board. The first student (1A or 1B) to unscramble the word wins the chance for his/her team to score points. If 1A wins the jumble, go to student 2A and give him/her a clue. He/she must give you the correct word which matches that clue. If he/she does, Team A scores a point, and you give student 3A a clue for which you expect another correct response. Continue giving Team A clues until some team member makes an incorrect response. An incorrect response sends the game back to the jumbled-word face off, this time with students 2A and 2B. Instead of repeating giving clues to the first few students of each team, continue with the student after the one who gave the last incorrect response on the team. For example, if Team B wins the jumbled-word face-off, and student 5B gave the last incorrect answer for Team B, you would start this round of clue questions with student 6B, and so on. The team with the most points wins!

UNIT TESTS

SHORT ANSWER UNIT TEST 1 - *The Stranger*

A. Identify:

___ 1. Celeste   A. Owns beach house

___ 2. Masson   B. Works with Meursault

___ 3. Meursault   C. Loves/hates his dog

___ 4. Raymond   D. Meursault's girlfriend

___ 5. Salamano   E. Says, "Nothing matters."

___ 6. Emmanuel   F. Mother's friend at the home

___ 7. Marie   G. Owns Restaurant

___ 8. Perez   H. Beats up his mistress

B. Short Answer:

1. What does Meursault do in the opening chapter?

2. What does Meursault do for Raymond?

3. Meursault tells his boss that "people never change their lives, that in any case one life is as good as another." What do we learn about Meursault from this statement?

Stranger Short Answer Unit Test 1 Page 2

4. Why does Meursault return to the beach and to the rock by the water?

5. What does Meursault do when he encounters the Arab at the rock? Why?

6. What about Meursault upsets and frustrates his lawyer and the magistrate?

7. How does Meursault pass his time in prison?

8. At Meursault's trial, why is so much made of his conduct at his mother's funeral?

The Stranger Short Answer Unit Test 1 Page 3

III. Essay:
    Explain why Meursault never repents or does anything to try to save himself.

IV. Vocabulary
    Listen to the vocabulary words and write them down. Go back later and fill in the correct definition for each word.

1.

2.

3.

4.

5.

6.

7.

8.

9.

10.

KEY: SHORT ANSWER UNIT TEST #1 - *The Stranger*

A. Identify:

_G_	1. Celeste	A. Owns beach house
_A_	2. Masson	B. Works with Meursault
_E_	3. Meursault	C. Loves/hates his dog
_H_	4. Raymond	D. Meursault's girlfriend
_C_	5. Salamano	E. Says, "Nothing matters."
_B_	6. Emmanuel	F. Mother's friend at the home
_D_	7. Marie	G. Owns Restaurant
_F_	8. Perez	H. Beats up his mistress

B. Short Answer:

1. What does Meursault do in the opening chapter?
    Informed of his mother's death, Meursault goes to the home for the aged where she has lived. He sits in vigil for her overnight and attends her burial the next day.

2. What does Meursault do for Raymond?
    He writes a letter to Raymond's mistress and later testifies to the police for him.

3. Meursault tells his boss that "people never change their lives, that in any case one life is as good as another." What do we learn about Meursault from this statement?
    It reflects Meursault's attitude that nothing matters. One life is as good as another; there is no good or bad, no right or wrong; things just are the way they are. Whether things are one way or another makes no difference. He doesn't judge Raymond or pity Salamano's dog, care whether or not he moves to Paris, or feel grief at his mother's death. He just takes everything with an indifferent attitude.

4. Why does Meursault return to the beach and to the rock by the water?
    He is too tired to climb the stairs to the beach house and to face the women. Since he thinks it makes no difference if he climbs the stairs or not, he decides to take the easy route and go back to the beach. As he walks, the sun becomes hotter and he heads back to the shade and cool

water by the rock.

5. What does Meursault do when he encounters the Arab at the rock? Why?
   He shoots him. The first shot was an accident; he was dazed by the sun, couldn't see because of the sweat in his eyes, and he pulled the trigger of the gun before he realized what he had done. The other four shots he fired into the corpse remain unexplained.

6. What about Meursault upsets and frustrates his lawyer and the magistrate?
   Meursault's lack of emotion or remorse concerning both his crime and his mother's death cause both his lawyer and the magistrate to become angry and unsure of how to deal with him.

7. How does Meursault pass his time in prison?
   He sleeps most of the time, and in the remaining hours, he tries to remember details of his room at home and does other mind games, and tends to things like meals and other events of the prison routine.

8. At Meursault's trial, why is so much made of his conduct at his mother's funeral?
   Meursault's lack of emotion at his own mother's funeral gives the prosecution evidence that Meursault is a hard-hearted man, a cold-blooded killer.

III. Essay: Answers will vary.
   Explain why Meursault never repents or does anything to try to save himself.

IV. Vocabulary Choose ten of the vocabulary words to read orally for Part IV of the unit test.

SHORT ANSWER UNIT TEST 2 - *The Stranger*

I. Matching

___ 1. Celeste   A. Works with Meursault

___ 2. Masson   B. Mother's friend at the home

___ 3. Meursault   C. Beats up his mistress

___ 4. Raymond   D. Says, "Nothing matters."

___ 5. Salamano   E. Owns Restaurant

___ 6. Emmanuel   F. Owns beach house

___ 7. Marie   G. Meursault's girlfriend

___ 8. Perez   H. Loves/hates his dog

II. Short Answer

1. What is Meursault's reaction to his mother's death? (1)

2. What insights do we gain into Meursault's character judging from his interactions with Salamano and Raymond? (3)

3. Why do the police come to Raymond's room? (4)

Stranger Short Answer Unit Test 2 Page 2

4. Meursault tells his boss that "people never change their lives, that in any case one life is as good as another." What do we learn about Meursault from this statement? (5)

5. Why does Meursault return to the beach and to the rock by the water? (6)

6. What about Meursault upsets and frustrates his lawyer and the magistrate? (1)

7. At Meursault's trial, why is so much made of his conduct at his mother's funeral? (3)

8. What is Marie's testimony and how does it hurt Meursault's case? (3)

9. What does Meursault try to explain to the chaplain after he becomes angry? (6)

Stranger Short Answer Unit Test 2 Page 3

III. Composition
    What characteristics of existentialism are present in *The Stranger*, and how is each shown?

Stranger Short Answer Unit Test 2 Page 4

IV. Vocabulary

    Listen to the vocabulary words and write them down. Go back later and fill in the correct definition for each word.

1.

2.

3.

4.

5.

6.

7.

8.

9.

10.

KEY: SHORT ANSWER UNIT TEST 2 *The Stranger*

I. Matching (Use this matching key for the Advanced Short Answer Unit Test, too.)

_E_	1. Celeste	A.	Works with Meursault
_F_	2. Masson	B.	Mother's friend at the home
_D_	3. Meursault	C.	Beats up his mistress
_C_	4. Raymond	D.	Says, "Nothing matters."
_H_	5. Salamano	E.	Owns Restaurant
_A_	6. Emmanuel	F.	Owns beach house
_G_	7. Marie	G.	Meursault's girlfriend
_B_	8. Perez	H.	Loves/hates his dog

II. Short Answer

1. What is Meursault's reaction to his mother's death? (1)
    He is emotionally unaffected by it. He goes through the motions of what is expected of him yet appears to be unconcerned. He does not weep or seem at all grieved at his mother's death.

2. What insights do we gain into Meursault's character judging from his interactions with Salamano and Raymond? (3)
    Meursault does not judge either man. As to the dog's life being pitiful, he just thinks, "Who's to say?" He listens to Raymond because he finds Raymond to be somewhat interesting and because he has no reason to not listen to him.

3. Why do the police come to Raymond's room? (4)
    A neighbor called the police to come because Raymond is beating his mistress. Note that although Marie asks Meursault to call the police, he refuses saying simply that he does not like the police.

4. Meursault tells his boss that "people never change their lives, that in any case one life is as good as another." What do we learn about Meursault from this statement? (5)
    It reflects Meursault's attitude that nothing matters. One life is as good as another; there is no good or bad, no right or wrong; things just are the way they are. Whether things are one way or

another makes no difference. He doesn't judge Raymond or pity Salamano's dog, care whether or not he moves to Paris, or feel grief at his mother's death. He just takes everything with an indifferent attitude.

5. Why does Meursault return to the beach and to the rock by the water? (6)
   He is too tired to climb the stairs to the beach house and to face the women. Since he thinks it makes no difference if he climbs the stairs or not, he decides to take the easy route and go back to the beach. As he walks, the sun becomes hotter and he heads back to the shade and cool water by the rock.

6. What about Meursault upsets and frustrates his lawyer and the magistrate? (1)
   Meursault's lack of emotion or remorse concerning both his crime and his mother's death cause both his lawyer and the magistrate to become angry and unsure of how to deal with him.

7. At Meursault's trial, why is so much made of his conduct at his mother's funeral? (3)
   Meursault's lack of emotion at his own mother's funeral gives the prosecution evidence that Meursault is a hard-hearted man, a cold-blooded killer.

8. What is Marie's testimony and how does it hurt Meursault's case? (3)
   She relates the events of the day they began their relationship -- their meeting at the beach, the movie, and their night together. Since these events took place on the day after his mother's funeral, they reinforce the prosecution's idea that Meursault is without morals; he is out having a good time, living it up at a time when he should be in mourning.

9. What does Meursault try to explain to the chaplain after he becomes angry? (6)
   He tries to make the chaplain see that one life is as good (or bad) as another, that everyone waits for his execution, that nothing matters because ultimately there is only "nothing."

III. Composition   Answers will vary.
   What characteristics of existentialism are present in *The Stranger*, and how is each shown?

IV. Vocabulary
   Choose ten of the vocabulary words to dictate to your students.

ADVANCED SHORT ANSWER UNIT TEST - *The Stranger*

I. Matching

___ 1. Celeste   A. Works with Meursault

___ 2. Masson   B. Mother's friend at the home

___ 3. Meursault   C. Beats up his mistress

___ 4. Raymond   D. Says, "Nothing matters."

___ 5. Salamano   E. Owns Restaurant

___ 6. Emmanuel   F. Owns beach house

___ 7. Marie   G. Meursault's girlfriend

___ 8. Perez   H. Loves/hates his dog

II. Short Answer

1. Compare and contrast Meursault and Raymond.

2. Compare and contrast the magistrate and the chaplain.

Stranger Advanced Short Answer Unit Test Page 2

3. What characteristics of existentialism are present in the novel, and how are they shown.

4. What is the function of the character of Marie in the novel?

5. Why did Meursault want a crowd of people at his execution?

Stranger Advanced Short Answer Unit Test Page 3

III. Composition

About *The Stranger*, Matthew Ward said, ". . . in the mind of a moralist, simplification is tantamount to immorality, and Meursault and Camus are each moralists in their own way. What little Meursault says or feels or does resonates with all he does not say, all he does not feel, all he does not do. The 'simplicity' of the text is merely apparent and everywhere paradoxical."

Defend this statement using examples from the text of *The Stranger*.

Stranger Advanced Short Answer Unit Test Page 4

IV. Vocabulary

Listen to the vocabulary words and write them down. Go back later and write a composition in which you use all of the words. The composition must relate in some way to *The Stranger*.

MULTIPLE CHOICE UNIT TEST 1 - *The Stranger*

I. Matching

___ 1. Celeste   A. Owns beach house

___ 2. Masson   B. Works with Meursault

___ 3. Meursault   C. Loves/hates his dog

___ 4. Raymond   D. Meursault's girlfriend

___ 5. Salamano   E. Says, "Nothing matters."

___ 6. Emmanuel   F. Mother's friend at the home

___ 7. Marie   G. Owns Restaurant

___ 8. Perez   H. Beats up his mistress

II. Multiple Choice

1. From what point of view is the novel written?
    a. It is written from the first person point of view.
    b. It is written from the third person point of view.
    c. It is written from the third person omniscient author point of view.

2. What is Meursault's reaction to his mother's death?
    a. He screams and cries, and has to be restrained.
    b. He is crushed, but bears his grief stoically.
    c. He says he never loved her anyway, and he is glad to be rid of her.
    d. He is emotionally unaffected, and doesn't weep or grieve.

3. What insights do we gain into Meursault's character from his interactions with Salamano and Raymond?
    a. He is harsh and judgmental.
    b. He does not judge either man.
    c. He uses people for his own advantage.
    d. He is insane.

Stranger Multiple Choice Unit Test 1 Page 2

4. Meursault tells his boss that "people never change their lives, that in any case one life is as good as another." What do we learn about Meursault from this statement?
    a. He is a philosopher.
    b. He takes everything with an indifferent attitude.
    c. He is not respectful to his superiors.
    d. He values life above all else.

5. How does Meursault respond when Marie asks if he loves her?
    a. He says it doesn't mean anything, but he probably doesn't love her.
    b. He says he loves her very much.
    c. He changes the subject.
    d. He tells her he loves her even though he doesn't, just because it's easier than telling the truth.

6. Why does Meursault go to the beach house?
    a. He wants to get away from Marie.
    b. He has been invited by Raymond.
    c. He has been evicted from his apartment and has nowhere else to go.
    d. He is thinking of buying it for an investment.

7. What does Meursault do when he encounters the man at the rock?
    a. He shoots him.
    b. He knifes him.
    c. He starts a fist fight.
    d. He strangles the man.

8. Does Meursault seem to care whether or not Marie comes back to visit him in jail?
    a. Yes, he does.
    b. No, he doesn't.

9. What does Celeste say concerning the murder?
    a. He says that he always thought Meursault had a violent streak.
    b. He said he was sure it was self-defense.
    c. He said it was bad luck.
    d. He said the Arab got what he deserved.

Stranger Multiple Choice Unit Test 1 Page 3

10. What does Meursault tell the chaplain?
    a. He says he has had a conversion and asks to be baptized.
    b. He says he does not believe in God and has no time for things that do not interest him.
    c. He is sorry for all he has done and asks for forgiveness.
    d. He wishes he could go back and do it all over again; he would do things differently.

11. What does Meursault do after the chaplain responds to his statement?
    a. He tries to make the chaplain see that nothing matters because ultimately there is only nothing.
    b. He kneels down and starts praying, and asks to be forgiven.
    c. He finally breaks down and laughs hysterically.
    d. He called for the guards and asked to have the chaplain removed.

III. True or False

_____ 1. Meursault loved Marie.

_____ 2. An existentialist would have great faith in God.

_____ 3. Meursault frequently lies.

_____ 4. Raymond tricked Meursault into killing the Arab.

_____ 5. Meursault may have loved his mother, but was unaffected by her death.

_____ 6. Keeping in mind the philosophy of existentialism upon which *The Stranger* is based, Meursault has to pay for his crime. There is no chance for a happy ending.

_____ 7. One concept in existentialism is the idea that man has no freedom of choice.

_____ 8. Albert Camus was a French priest who wrote to try to help people improve themselves.

_____ 9. Meursault repented for his wrongdoings, but an in an indifferent world his fate could not be changed.

_____ 10. Marie testified at Meursault's trial, but her testimony hurt more than it helped his case.

_____ 11. The magistrate and the chaplain had exactly the same attitude towards Meursault; they approached him in exactly the same way.

_____ 12. *The Stranger* is divided into two parts: the first part deals mostly with the inner workings of Meursault's mind. The second part deals mostly with the outside world.

The Stranger Multiple Choice Unit Test 1 Page 4

IV. Vocabulary   Match the correct definitions to the words.

1. VAGUE   A. Endless; tiresome

2. ADJOURNED   B. Freed from a charge or accusation

3. HEINOUS   C. Filthy; dirty; foul; morally degraded

4. OASIS   D. Easily seen or understood

5. INDIGNANTLY   E. With anger aroused by something unjust

6. ACQUITTED   F. Can't be ruffled; unshakably calm and collected

7. TIRADE   G. Stringy and tough; lean and muscular

8. ODIOUS   H. A long, angry or violent speech

9. CONVICTION   I. Arousing feelings of dislike, aversion or displeasure

10. CORDIAL   J. A place preserved from surrounding unpleasantness; a refuge

11. PROMONTORY   K. Suspended until a later stated time

12. SINEWY   L. The murdering of one's parents or other close relatives

13. IMPERTURBABLE   M. Warm and sincere; friendly

14. PLAUSIBLE   N. Horrible; wicked

15. PARRICIDE   O. Burning; hot; fire-like

16. FIERY   P. Belief

17. INTERMINABLE   Q. Believable

18. OBVIOUS   R. High ridge of land or rock jutting into the water

19. SORDID   S. Subdued; inhibited; held back

20. SUPPRESSED   T. Not clearly expressed; not distinct

MULTIPLE CHOICE UNIT TEST 2 - *The Stranger*

I. Matching

___ 1. Celeste   A. Works with Meursault

___ 2. Masson   B. Mother's friend at the home

___ 3. Meursault   C. Beats up his mistress

___ 4. Raymond   D. Says, "Nothing matters."

___ 5. Salamano   E. Owns Restaurant

___ 6. Emmanuel   F. Owns beach house

___ 7. Marie   G. Meursault's girlfriend

___ 8. Perez   H. Loves/hates his dog

II. Multiple Choice

1. From what point of view is the novel written?
    a. It is written from the third person omniscient author point of view.
    b. It is written from the first person point of view.
    c. It is written from the third person point of view.

2. What is Meursault's reaction to his mother's death?
    a. He is emotionally unaffected, and doesn't weep or grieve.
    b. He screams and cries, and has to be restrained.
    c. He says he never loved her anyway, and he is glad to be rid of her.
    d. He is crushed, but bears his grief stoically.

3. What insights do we gain into Meursault's character from his interactions with Salamano and Raymond?
    a. He uses people for his own advantage.
    b. He is harsh and judgmental.
    c. He does not judge either man.
    d. He is insane.

Stranger Multiple Choice Unit Test 2 Page 2

4. Meursault tells his boss that "people never change their lives, that in any case one life is as good as another." What do we learn about Meursault from this statement?
    a. He is not respectful to his superiors.
    b. He is a philosopher.
    c. He values life above all else.
    d. He takes everything with an indifferent attitude.

5. How does Meursault respond when Marie asks if he loves her?
    a. He changes the subject.
    b. He says it doesn't mean anything, but he probably doesn't love her.
    c. He tells her he loves her even though he doesn't, just because it's easier than telling the truth.
    d. He says he loves her very much.

6. Why does Meursault go to the beach house?
    a. He is thinking of buying it for an investment.
    b. He wants to get away from Marie.
    c. He has been evicted from his apartment and has nowhere else to go.
    d. He has been invited by Raymond.

7. What does Meursault do when he encounters the man at the rock?
    a. He strangles the man.
    b. He knifes him.
    c. He shoots him.
    d. He starts a fist fight.

8. Does Meursault seem to care whether or not Marie comes back to visit him in jail?
    a. Yes, he does.
    b. No, he doesn't.

9. What does Celeste say concerning the murder?
    a. He said it was bad luck.
    b. He says that he always thought Meursault had a violent streak.
    c. He said he was sure it was self-defense.
    d. He said the Arab got what he deserved.

Stranger Multiple Choice Unit Test 2 Page 3

10. What does Meursault tell the chaplain?
    a. He is sorry for all he has done and asks for forgiveness.
    b. He says he has had a conversion and asks to be baptized.
    c. He wishes he could go back and do it all over again; he would do things differently.
    d. He says he does not believe in God and has no time for things that do not interest him.

11. What does Meursault do after the chaplain responds to his statement?
    a. He called for the guards and asked to have the chaplain removed.
    b. He tries to make the chaplain see that nothing matters because ultimately there is only nothing.
    c. He kneels down and starts praying, and asks to be forgiven.
    d. He finally breaks down and laughs hysterically.

III. Composition

Matthew Ward said, "As he [Meursault] says toward the end of his story, as he sees things, Salamano's dog was worth just as much as Salamano's wife. Such peculiarities of perception, such psychological increments of character *are* Meursault."

Explain what Mr. Ward meant using other examples from *The Stranger*.

The Stranger Multiple Choice Unit Test 2 Page 4

IV. Vocabulary   Match the correct definitions to the words.

____ 1. PROPOSITION   A. Doubtful

____ 2. PALL   B. High ridge of land or rock jutting into the water

____ 3. OASIS   C. Poor; impoverished

____ 4. PROMONTORY   D. Sneaky; stealthy

____ 5. PECULIAR   E. Subdued; inhibited; held back

____ 6. INCOHERENTLY   F. Proposal; a plan suggested for approval

____ 7. DUBIOUS   G. To express disapproval or criticism

____ 8. PREMEDITATED   H. Afternoon (theater) performances

____ 9. DESTITUTE   I. Unusual; odd

____ 10. REPROACH   J. Coffin cover

____ 11. FURTIVE   K. Spoil; corrupt

____ 12. PRECISELY   L. A place preserved from surrounding unpleasantness; a refuge

____ 13. SUPPRESSED   M. One who does not believe in God

____ 14. HEINOUS   N. Without connections; in an unclear or unorderly manner

____ 15. MATINEES   O. Exactly

____ 16. TAINT   P. Unavoidable; impossible to prevent

____ 17. CORDIAL   Q. Horrible; wicked

____ 18. ATHEIST   R. Planned beforehand

____ 19. INEVITABLE   S. Warm and sincere; friendly

____ 20. IMPERTURBABLE   T. Can't be ruffled; unshakably calm and collected

ANSWER SHEET - *The Stranger*
Multiple Choice Unit Tests

I. Matching	II. Multiple Choice	III. True/False	IV. Vocabulary
1. ___	1. ___	1. ___	1. ___
2. ___	2. ___	2. ___	2. ___
3. ___	3. ___	3. ___	3. ___
4. ___	4. ___	4. ___	4. ___
5. ___	5. ___	5. ___	5. ___
6. ___	6. ___	6. ___	6. ___
7. ___	7. ___	7. ___	7. ___
8. ___	8. ___	8. ___	8. ___
	9. ___	9. ___	9. ___
	10. ___	10. ___	10. ___
	11. ___	11. ___	11. ___
		12. ___	12. ___
			13. ___
			14. ___
			15. ___
			16. ___
			17. ___
			18. ___
			19. ___
			20. ___

ANSWER KEY MULTIPLE CHOICE UNIT TESTS – *The Stranger*

Answers to Unit Test 1 are in the left column. Answers to Unit Test 2 are in the right column.
True/False is in test 1 only.

I. Matching	II. Multiple Choice	III. True/False	IV. Vocabulary
1. G E	1. A B	1. False	1. T F
2. A F	2. D A	2. False	2. K J
3. E D	3. B C	3. False	3. N L
4. H C	4. B D	4. False	4. J B
5. C H	5. A B	5. True	5. E I
6. B A	6. B D	6. True	6. B N
7. D G	7. A C	7. False	7. H A
8. F B	8. B B	8. False	8. I R
	9. C A	9. False	9. P C
	10. B D	10. True	10. M G
	11. A B	11. False	11. R D
		12. False	12. G O
			13. F E
			14. Q Q
			15. L H
			16. O K
			17. A S
			18. D M
			19. C P
			20. S T

UNIT RESOURCE MATERIALS

BULLETIN BOARD IDEAS - *The Stranger*

1. Save one corner of the board for the best of student's *The Stranger* writing assignments.

2. Take one of the word search puzzles from the extra activities and with a marker copy it over in a large size on the bulletin board. Write the clue words to find to one side. Invite students prior to and after class to find the words and circle them on the bulletin board.

3. If your bulletin board is easily seen by all students, write up the vocabulary words and definitions for students to look at in their spare time.

4. Make a bulletin board listing the vocabulary words for this unit. As you complete sections of the novel and discuss the vocabulary for each section, write the definitions on the bulletin board. (If your board is one students face frequently, it will help them learn the words.)

5. Title the board THE STRANGER. In the center of the board, write out the definition of the word "existentialism." From each part of the definition, run out a piece of yarn to a written-out example of that part of the definition. For example from "responsibility for the consequences of his acts" send a string of yarn to a colorful piece of construction paper with the words, "Meursault is found guilty and is sentenced to death." And so on, for each part of the definition.

6. Title the board THE STRANGER. Post these quotes from the novel on colorful construction paper or write them on your background paper with colorful markers:
    "Mother died today. Or maybe yesterday; I can't be sure."
    "Who's to say?"
    "I don't have any reason not to talk to him."
    "It didn't mean anything."
    "One life is as good as another."
    "I had only to wish that there be a large crowd of spectators the day of my execution and that they greet me with cries of hate."

    Around these quotes, place pictures of things and scenes in the story: the glaring sun, the beach, the ocean, a gun, a beach house, a chaplain, jail, a courtroom, etc.

EXTRA ACTIVITIES - *The Stranger*

One of the difficulties in teaching a novel is that all students don't read at the same speed. One student who likes to read may take the book home and finish it in a day or two. Sometimes a few students finish the in-class assignments early. The problem, then, is finding suitable extra activities for students.

The best thing I've found is to keep a little library in the classroom. For this unit on *The Stranger*, you might check out from the school library other related books and articles about philosophy, the justice system, careers in the justice system, jury duty, treatment of the elderly in various societies, conditions in nursing homes, the death penalty, or articles of criticism about *The Stranger*. A biography of Albert Camus would be interesting for some students to read. Other works by Albert Camus would also make good additions to your in-class library.

Other things you may keep on hand are puzzles. We have made some relating directly to *The Stranger* for you. Feel free to duplicate them for your students.

Some students may like to draw. You might devise a contest or allow some extra-credit grade for students who draw characters or scenes from *The Stranger*. Note, too, that if the students do not want to keep their drawings you may pick up some extra bulletin board materials this way. If you have a contest and you supply the prize (a CD or something like that perhaps), you could, possibly, make the drawing itself a non-returnable entry fee.

The pages which follow contain games, puzzles and worksheets. The keys, when appropriate, immediately follow the puzzle or worksheet. There are two main groups of activities: one group for the unit; that is, generally relating to *The Stranger* text, and another group of activities related strictly to *The Stranger* vocabulary.

Directions for these games, puzzles and worksheets are self-explanatory. The object here is to provide you with extra materials you may use in any way you choose.

MORE ACTIVITIES - *The Stranger*

1. Pick a chapter or scene and have the students act it out on a stage. (Perhaps you could assign various scenes to different groups of students so more than one scene could be acted and more students could participate.)

2. Have a guest speaker come in to talk with students about coping with death and grief.

3. Use some of the related topics noted earlier in the unit as topics for guest speakers or research papers.

4. Have students design a book cover (front and back and inside flaps) for *The Stranger*.

5. Have students design a bulletin board (ready to be put up; not just sketched) for *The Stranger*.

6. Have students act out the trial of Meursault. They could either follow the one in the text closely or they could hold their own trial of Meursault.

7. Do a mini-philosophy unit in which you expose students to many different kinds of philosophies.

8. Take a field trip to a nursing home or senior citizen center to show students what they are really like.

WORD SEARCH - *The Stranger*

All words in this list are associated with *The Stranger* with an emphasis on the vocabulary words chosen for study in the text. The words are placed backwards, forward, diagonally, up and down. The included words are listed below.

```
A J W V Y Z H M K F R Y M Z G G J G J L W R T Y
T R P B Y D K D E J D A S J N U Z G N C M R M C
N C A E Y Q E Z Z U S C Y E Q L I G M I I G G G
L C X B R C C M F S R Q T M S M E L N A H S S V
P E E L S E I V O M N S C D O K C U L E T T E R
C B S U L A Z N N C E L A T O N S N N O R R O C
G C M L V L L X L L K P H U N G D R O A T Q D N
M A R I E I I A E V D E G V L V N H N F M I H M
C N W W S F S C M C R U Y V K T S G X S Z M N X
S V P Z I J Y I P A I Z C P N Q E F F N D Y E E
H V H C B R C D T L N L P M W R X X S F P H W T
F D U H C A E B T F L O O R E M O R S E F P W T
Z R F B F F F Y Q F L B S P Y H Y K Q F Q G K C
C M V V I Y R D W P Z C Z W V B L Q Q N J G H K
R Z T L Z K J T K A W R R G M B M D X C H X Q K
Z N W S N V T L R Q L P C S M V T X Q M N X F T
S Q J V Z M C D S K C X S W Y D N Y J J K L S P
N N L W L Z H M X C N W M L S K L S H Y X C S T
T P L H C B N G K S P P J Z K P T K J G B F L F
V V Q B C S D Y J Q R M C S H G G S Y Z F W Z B
```

ARABS	GOD	MEURSAULT	SHOOTS
BEACH	GUILLOTINE	MOTHER	SLEEP
CAMUS	GUILTY	MOVIES	STRANGER
CELESTE	LAWYER	NOTHING	SUN
CELL	LETTER	PEREZ	TRIAL
COMEDY	LIFE	POLICE	VISIT
CRUCIFIX	LUCK	RAYMOND	
DOG	MARIE	REMORSE	
EMMANUEL	MASSON	SALAMANO	

KEY WORD SEARCH - *The Stranger*

All words in this list are associated with *The Stranger* with an emphasis on the vocabulary words chosen for study in the text. The words are placed backwards, forward, diagonally, up and down. The included words are listed below.

```
           A        Y        M           R        M    G         G               T
             R  P        D        E           A         U        N         R
               A  E         E         U  S     Y  E     L  I        I  I
                 B  R      C  M        S  R      T  M    M  E  L  N  A  H  S  S
           P  E  E  L  S  E  I  V  O  M     S        D  O  K  C  U  L  E  T  T  E  R
                 U  L  A  Z  N        C  E     A  T  O  N  S        N  O  R         O
               M  L  V     L  X     L        H  U     G  D     O  A  T            N
           M  A  R  I  E  I  I  A  E        E  G     L        H  N     M  I
           C              F  S  C  M  C  R  U           T  S  G           M  N
                       I        I     A  I                 E                    E  E
                    C        R        T  L  N  L           R
              U  H  C  A  E  B  T        O  O  R  E  M  O  R  S  E
           R              F        Y                    P
           C           I              W
                    L                    A
                                         L
```

ARABS	GOD	MEURSAULT	SHOOTS
BEACH	GUILLOTINE	MOTHER	SLEEP
CAMUS	GUILTY	MOVIES	STRANGER
CELESTE	LAWYER	NOTHING	SUN
CELL	LETTER	PEREZ	TRIAL
COMEDY	LIFE	POLICE	VISIT
CRUCIFIX	LUCK	RAYMOND	
DOG	MARIE	REMORSE	
EMMANUEL	MASSON	SALAMANO	

CROSSWORD - *The Stranger*

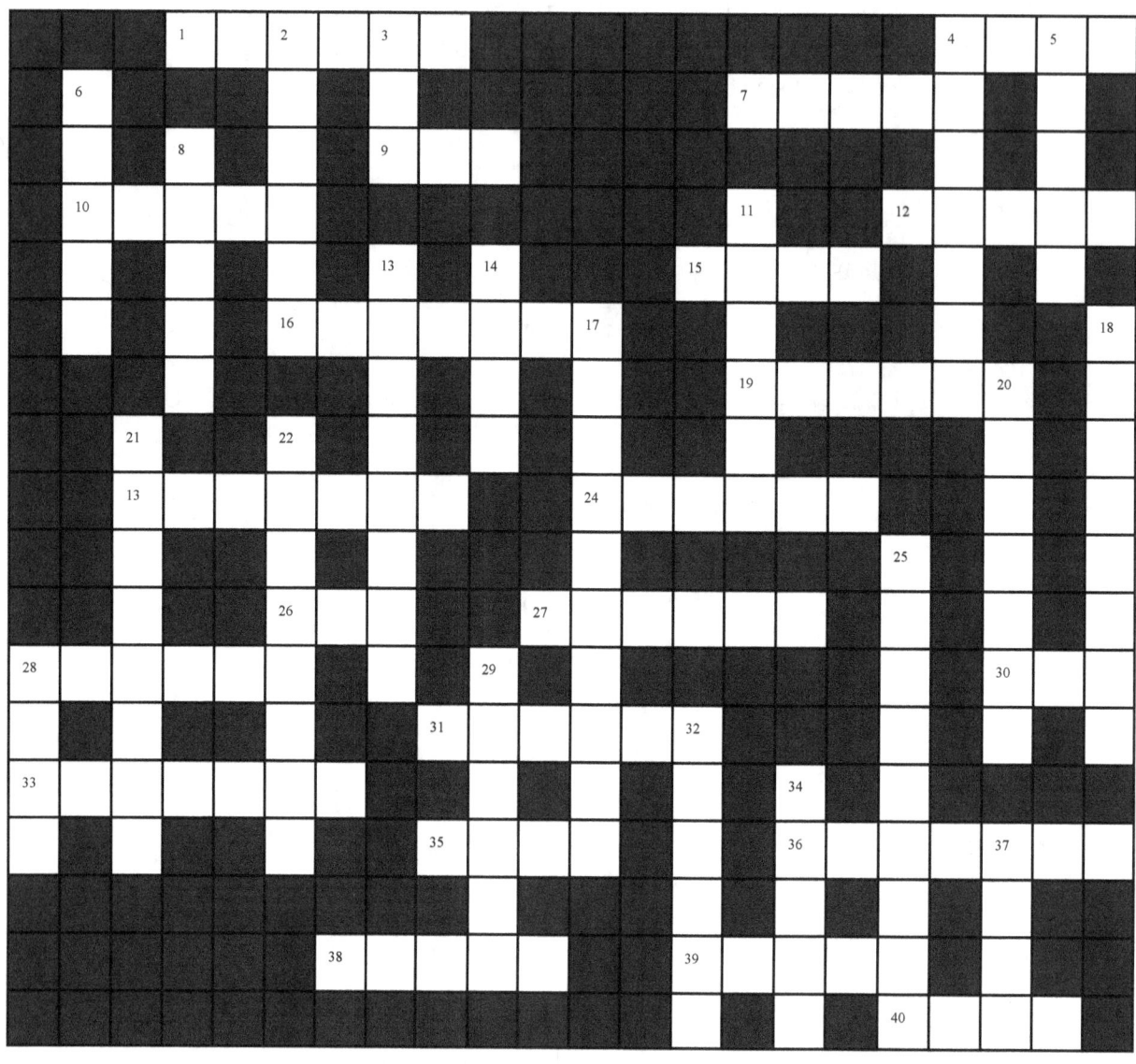

CROSSWORD CLUES - *The Stranger*

ACROSS
1. Kind of movie Meursault and Marie watched
4. Jail cubicle
7. Meursault's girlfriend
9. Meursault tells the chaplain he doesn't believe in __.
10. They cut Raymond
12. Mother's friend at the home
15. Celeste called the murder 'bad ___'
16. Nothing matters because ultimately, there is only ____
19. Raymond wanted Meursault to write one for him
23. Beats up mistress
24. Attorney
26. Present plural of 'to be'; we ---
27. Meursault attends her funeral
28. Jail
30. It was hot and glaring
31. Meursault & Marie go there after the beach on their first date
33. One who grieves
35. Pleasing and agreeable in nature
36. See in one's mind's eye
38. It takes up most of Meursault's prison time
39. Process by which guilt or innocence is determined
40. Opposite of this

DOWN
2. Owns beach house
3. Salamano's pet
4. Owns restaurant
5. One who likes to be alone
6. Place where Meursault meets Marie
8. Author
11. The verdict
13. The ____
14. Meursault says, 'one ___ is as good as another.'
17. Method of execution
18. Loves/hates his dog
20. Meursault's lack of ___ upsets his lawyer & the magistrate
21. Magistrate waves one in front of Meursault
22. Works with Meursault
25. Says, 'Nothing matters.'
28. That on which words are printed in a book
29. A neighbor calls them to come to Raymond's room
32. Meursault ___ the Arab
34. Marie went to ___ Meursault in jail
37. A thought

CROSSWORD ANSWER KEY - *The Stranger*

MATCHING QUIZ/WORKSHEET 1 - *The Stranger*

____ 1. POLICE   A. Owns beach house

____ 2. REMORSE   B. Raymond wanted Meursault to write one for him

____ 3. GOD   C. Magistrate waves one in front of Meursault

____ 4. SALAMANO   D. Loves/hates his dog

____ 5. GUILLOTINE   E. Meursault tells the chaplain he doesn't believe in ___

____ 6. CRUCIFIX   F. A neighbor calls them to come to Raymond's room

____ 7. MOTHER   G. Jail cubicle

____ 8. SHOOTS   H. Owns restaurant

____ 9. MARIE   I. Celeste called the murder 'bad ___'

____ 10. CELESTE   J. Works with Meursault

____ 11. STRANGER   K. Process by which guilt or innocence is determined

____ 12. EMMANUEL   L. Kind of movie Meursault and Marie watched

____ 13. MASSON   M. Method of execution

____ 14. RAYMOND   N. Meursault attends her funeral

____ 15. CELL   O. Meursault ___ the Arab

____ 16. LETTER   P. Meursault's girlfriend

____ 17. COMEDY   Q. The ____

____ 18. TRIAL   R. It was hot and glaring

____ 19. LUCK   S. Meursault's lack of ___ upsets his lawyer & the magistrate

____ 20. SUN   T. Beats up mistress

KEY: MATCHING QUIZ/WORKSHEET 1 - *The Stranger*

__F__	1. POLICE	A. Owns beach house
__S__	2. REMORSE	B. Raymond wanted Meursault to write one for him
__E__	3. GOD	C. Magistrate waves one in front of Meursault
__D__	4. SALAMANO	D. Loves/hates his dog
__M__	5. GUILLOTINE	E. Meursault tells the chaplain he doesn't believe in ___
__C__	6. CRUCIFIX	F. A neighbor calls them to come to Raymond's room
__N__	7. MOTHER	G. Jail cubicle
__O__	8. SHOOTS	H. Owns restaurant
__P__	9. MARIE	I. Celeste called the murder 'bad ___'
__H__	10. CELESTE	J. Works with Meursault
__Q__	11. STRANGER	K. Process by which guilt or innocence is determined
__J__	12. EMMANUEL	L. Kind of movie Meursault and Marie watched
__A__	13. MASSON	M. Method of execution
__T__	14. RAYMOND	N. Meursault attends her funeral
__G__	15. CELL	O. Meursault ___ the Arab
__B__	16. LETTER	P. Meursault's girlfriend
__L__	17. COMEDY	Q. The ___
__K__	18. TRIAL	R. It was hot and glaring
__I__	19. LUCK	S. Meursault's lack of ___ upsets his lawyer & the magistrate
__R__	20. SUN	T. Beats up mistress

MATCHING QUIZ/WORKSHEET 2 - *The Stranger*

____ 1. VISIT   A. Jail cubicle

____ 2. COMEDY   B. The verdict

____ 3. SUN   C. Marie went to ___ Meursault in jail

____ 4. MOTHER   D. Salamano's pet

____ 5. SHOOTS   E. Place where Meursault meets Marie

____ 6. TRIAL   F. It was hot and glaring

____ 7. RAYMOND   G. Meursault ___ the Arab

____ 8. CELESTE   H. The ____

____ 9. CRUCIFIX   I. Nothing matters because ultimately, there is only ____

____ 10. ARABS   J. Meursault's girlfriend

____ 11. GUILTY   K. Process by which guilt or innocence is determined

____ 12. CELL   L. Magistrate waves one in front of Meursault

____ 13. MEURSAULT   M. Says, 'Nothing matters.'

____ 14. MASSON   N. Owns restaurant

____ 15. STRANGER   O. Owns beach house

____ 16. POLICE   P. They cut Raymond

____ 17. DOG   Q. Beats up mistress

____ 18. MARIE   R. Kind of movie Meursault and Marie watched

____ 19. BEACH   S. Meursault attends her funeral

____ 20. NOTHING   T. A neighbor calls them to come to Raymond's room

KEY: MATCHING QUIZ/WORKSHEET 2 - *The Stranger*

_C_	1. VISIT	A. Jail cubicle
_R_	2. COMEDY	B. The verdict
_F_	3. SUN	C. Marie went to ___ Meursault in jail
_S_	4. MOTHER	D. Salamano's pet
_G_	5. SHOOTS	E. Place where Meursault meets Marie
_K_	6. TRIAL	F. It was hot and glaring
_Q_	7. RAYMOND	G. Meursault ___ the Arab
_N_	8. CELESTE	H. The ____
_L_	9. CRUCIFIX	I. Nothing matters because ultimately, there is only ____
_P_	10. ARABS	J. Meursault's girlfriend
_B_	11. GUILTY	K. Process by which guilt or innocence is determined
_A_	12. CELL	L. Magistrate waves one in front of Meursault
_M_	13. MEURSAULT	M. Says, 'Nothing matters.'
_O_	14. MASSON	N. Owns restaurant
_H_	15. STRANGER	O. Owns beach house
_T_	16. POLICE	P. They cut Raymond
_D_	17. DOG	Q. Beats up mistress
_J_	18. MARIE	R. Kind of movie Meursault and Marie watched
_E_	19. BEACH	S. Meursault attends her funeral
_I_	20. NOTHING	T. A neighbor calls them to come to Raymond's room

JUGGLE LETTER REVIEW GAME CLUE SHEET - *The Stranger*

SCRAMBLED	WORD	CLUE
RSABA	ARABS	They cut Raymond
BCHEA	BEACH	Place where Meursault meets Marie
UACMS	CAMUS	Author
CLSTEEE	CELESTE	Owns restaurant
LCEL	CELL	Jail cubicle
COEDMY	COMEDY	Kind of movie Meursault and Marie watched
CUIRICXF	CRUCIFIX	Magistrate waves one in front of Meursault
GOD	DOG	Salamano's pet
MLMNEAUE	EMMANUEL	Works with Meursault
OGD	GOD	Meursault tells the chaplain he doesn't believe in __
GELILOTINU	GUILLOTINE	Method of execution
UIGYTL	GUILTY	The verdict
LRAEWY	LAWYER	Attorney
LREETT	LETTER	Raymond wanted Meursault to write one for him
FILE	LIFE	Meursault says, 'one ___ is as good as another.'
KLCU	LUCK	Celeste called the murder 'bad ___'
REAMI	MARIE	Meursault's girlfriend
SOANSM	MASSON	Owns beach house
ETMULURAS	MEURSAULT	Says, 'Nothing matters.'
MRTHOE	MOTHER	Meursault attends her funeral
VIEOMS	MOVIES	Meursault & Marie go there after the beach on their first date
GONHTNI	NOTHING	Nothing matters because ultimately, there is only __
ZEREP	PEREZ	Mother's friend at the home
PELIOC	POLICE	A neighbor calls them to come to Raymond's room
OYRAMDN	RAYMOND	Beats up mistress
ERMSROE	REMORSE	Meursault's lack of ___ upsets his lawyer & the magistrate
OSLANAMA	SALAMANO	Loves/hates his dog
SOTOHS	SHOOTS	Meursault ___ the Arab
PELES	SLEEP	It takes up most of Meursault's prison time
REGRNATS	STRANGER	The ____
UNS	SUN	It was hot and glaring
LARTI	TRIAL	Process by which guilt or innocence is determined
SIVTI	VISIT	Marie went to ___ Meursault in jail

VOCABULARY RESOURCE MATERIALS

VOCABULARY WORD SEARCH - *The Stranger*

All words in this list are associated with *The Stranger* with an emphasis on the vocabulary words chosen for study in the text. The words are placed backwards, forward, diagonally, up and down. The included words are listed below.

```
R D P L A U S I B L E T X C O N D O L E N C E S
N H E V I S L U P E R Y S Z D Z J P H A F Q B Q
C O N S U M M A T E D A R I T M A T I N E E S M
W C S Q T E P Y D V L Y F H E F C X A L B Z D P
L F S I E I F L L U A B W I C H C O B I Y I E H
T V H K A F T L A E B G A V E N T A R E N C Z F
V I G I L I B U T C S I U B S R T A D D U T L X
D Y N C S S L N T U A I O E R I Y I I L I L N C
R S W C U M A S O E N B C U V U C C I B A A M M
C H U O O S M I W B C Y L E S I T A D P M X L S
N O I O S H V B D I L J N E R M R R S I N E W Y
Z D N E N B E I R T D I J R E P H E E M D F W A
O D C V O I P R N A F E A N D C D W P P U R D J
X N J A U Z E A E D N P T E T I P S E R M J O D
I R S C P L N H L N I D M T W J S Q T L O I F S
H I L C E G S H B L T C I S I P W I P U C A G R
S M X V I S X I B L O L A S R U V Y R X S V C F
C Q A D W N H F O T B R Y T H E Q N M X Q Z N H
D N N Y S U O M Y N O N A P E E E C K V G X Z S
T I M P E R C E P T I B L Y X D D Y A X M Y Y R
```

ACQUITTED	FURTIVE	MATINEES	REPULSIVE
ADJOURNED	HEINOUS	MEEK	RESPITE
ANONYMOUS	IMPERCEPTIBLY	OASIS	SINEWY
ATHEIST	IMPERTURBABLE	OBVIOUS	SORDID
BRANDISHED	IMPLACABLE	ODIOUS	TAINT
CONDOLENCES	INCESSANT	PALL	TIRADE
CONSUMMATED	INCOHERENTLY	PALLOR	VAGUE
CONVULSION	INDICTMENT	PARRICIDE	VIGIL
CORDIAL	INDIGNANTLY	PECULIAR	VINDICATED
DESTITUTE	INEVITABLE	PLAUSIBLE	ZEAL
DUBIOUS	IRRELEVANT	PRECISELY	
FIERY	LIAISON	REPROACH	

KEY: VOCABULARY WORD SEARCH - *The Stranger*

All words in this list are associated with *The Stranger* with an emphasis on the vocabulary words chosen for study in the text. The words are placed backwards, forward, diagonally, up and down. The included words are listed below.

```
      D P L A U S I B L E T   C O N D O L E N C E S
    N   E V I S L U P E R   S               A
    C O N S U M M A T E D A R I T M A T I N E E S
      S   T E P Y D V L   F   E   C   A L   Z   P
      I E I   L L U A B   I   H   O B   I   E
      K A   T   A E B G A   E   T A R E N C
  V I G I L I   U T C S I U B   R T A D D U T L
      N     S L N T U A I O E R I Y I I L I L
      S   C U   A   O E   B C U V U C C I   A A
  C   U O O S   I     Y L E S I T A D P     L
      O I O S H V B   I L   N E R M R R S I N E W Y
      D N E N B E I R T D I   R E P   E E   D F   A
    O   C V O I P R N A   E A N         P P U R D
      N   A U   E A E D N P T E T I P S E R M J O
    I   S     L N H L N I D   T       T   O I   S
        I     E G S     L T C I   I     I U   A
    S     V I     I     O L A S   U V   R       C
          A D         O     R Y T H E Q N         H
        N N   S U O M Y N O N A   E E E C
          T I M P E R C E P T I B L Y   D D   A
```

ACQUITTED	FURTIVE	MATINEES	REPULSIVE
ADJOURNED	HEINOUS	MEEK	RESPITE
ANONYMOUS	IMPERCEPTIBLY	OASIS	SINEWY
ATHEIST	IMPERTURBABLE	OBVIOUS	SORDID
BRANDISHED	IMPLACABLE	ODIOUS	TAINT
CONDOLENCES	INCESSANT	PALL	TIRADE
CONSUMMATED	INCOHERENTLY	PALLOR	VAGUE
CONVULSION	INDICTMENT	PARRICIDE	VIGIL
CORDIAL	INDIGNANTLY	PECULIAR	VINDICATED
DESTITUTE	INEVITABLE	PLAUSIBLE	ZEAL
DUBIOUS	IRRELEVANT	PRECISELY	
FIERY	LIAISON	REPROACH	

VOCABULARY CROSSWORD - *The Stranger*

VOCABULARY CROSSWORD CLUES - *The Stranger*

ACROSS
1. In such a way as to be impossible to perceive by the senses
6. Celeste called the murder 'bad ___'
9. Expressions of sympathy or comfort
11. Spoil; corrupt
13. Jail cubicle
14. It was hot and glaring
15. Sneaky; stealthy
16. Affirmative response
17. Comprehend words on a page; --- a book
19. Freed from a charge or accusation
21. Shut
22. Feeling too high in temperature
23. To repose in a chair
24. Meursault's girlfriend
25. Salamano's pet
26. Doubtful
29. Link; a means of communication between different groups
31. Movement of ocean waters due to the moon's influence
32. Burning; hot; fire-like
34. They cut Raymond
35. Raymond wanted Meursault to write one for him
36. Filthy; dirty; foul; morally degraded
38. That's all; there is no more; the ---
41. Interested in other people's business
42. It takes up most of Meursault's prison time
44. Extreme or unnatural paleness
45. Not clearly expressed; not distinct
46. Enthusiastic devotion to a cause or an ideal
47. Mild; gentle; submissive
48. To cause to lie down; put down
49. Horrible; wicked

DOWN
2. Coffin cover
3. Move swiftly on foot
4. Sight organ
5. Came between
6. Meursault says, 'one ___ is as good as another'
7. Having an unknown or unacknowledged name
8. One who does not believe in God
9. Belief
10. Brought to completion or fruition; fulfilled
12. An intense involuntary muscular contraction; violent turmoil
13. Warm and sincere; friendly
18. Poor; impoverished
19. Suspended until a later stated time
20. A long, angry or violent speech
27. Waved or flourished; displayed
28. A place preserved from surrounding unpleasantness; a refuge
30. Impossible to please
33. Continuous without interruption
36. Stringy and tough; lean and muscular
37. A short rest; a temporary suspension of a death sentence
39. A watch
40. Meursault tells the chaplain he doesn't believe in ___
43. Mother's friend at the home

VOCABULARY CROSSWORD ANSWER KEY - *The Stranger*

VOCABULARY WORKSHEET 1 - *The Stranger*

____ 1. Brought to completion or fruition; fulfilled
    A. Consummated   B. Fiery   C. Meek   D. Convulsion

____ 2. Proposal; a plan suggested for approval
    A. Adjourned   B. Promontory   C. Sinewy   D. Proposition

____ 3. Freed from a charge or accusation
    A. Acquitted   B. Plausible   C. Repulsive   D. Indictment

____ 4. Not clearly expressed; not distinct
    A. Zeal   B. Imperceptibly   C. Vague   D. Obvious

____ 5. Extreme or unnatural paleness
    A. Plausible   B. Exaggerate   C. Pallor   D. Acquitted

____ 6. A short rest; a temporary suspension of a death sentence
    A. Repulsive   B. Respite   C. Proposition   D. Matinees

____ 7. Horrible; wicked
    A. Heinous   B. Destitute   C. Imperturbable   D. Adjourned

____ 8. Having an unknown or unacknowledged name
    A. Anonymous   B. Meek   C. Inevitable   D. Suppressed

____ 9. Exactly
    A. Anonymous   B. Precisely   C. Dubious   D. Intervened

____ 10. Unusual; odd
    A. Peculiar   B. Inevitable   C. Precisely   D. Irrelevant

____ 11. To express disapproval or criticism
    A. Vindicated   B. Promontory   C. Reproach   D. Suppressed

____ 12. Mild; gentle; submissive
    A. Respite   B. Meek   C. Pallor   D. Inevitable

____ 13. Spoil; corrupt
    A. Tirade   B. Imperceptibly   C. Taint   D. Incessant

____ 14. Without connections; in an unclear or unorderly manner
    A. Incoherently   B. Acquitted   C. Vindicated   D. Obvious

____ 15. Arousing feelings of dislike, aversion or displeasure
    A. Zeal   B. Premeditated   C. Proposition   D. Odious

____ 16. A place preserved from surrounding unpleasantness; a refuge
    A. Oasis   B. Zeal   C. Suppressed   D. Heinous

____ 17. Poor; impoverished
    A. Destitute   B. Odious   C. Consummated   D. Taint

____ 18. Filthy; dirty; foul; morally degraded
    A. Matinees   B. Sordid   C. Cordial   D. Tirade

____ 19. Link; a means of communication between different groups
    A. Liaison   B. Indignantly   C. Precisely   D. Zeal

____ 20. In such a way as to be impossible to perceive by the senses
    A. Consummated   B. Liaison   C. Imperceptibly   D. Dubious

KEY: VOCABULARY WORKSHEET 1 - *The Stranger*

_A_ 1. Brought to completion or fruition; fulfilled
  A. Consummated B. Fiery C. Meek D. Convulsion

_D_ 2. Proposal; a plan suggested for approval
  A. Adjourned B. Promontory C. Sinewy D. Proposition

_A_ 3. Freed from a charge or accusation
  A. Acquitted B. Plausible C. Repulsive D. Indictment

_C_ 4. Not clearly expressed; not distinct
  A. Zeal B. Imperceptibly C. Vague D. Obvious

_C_ 5. Extreme or unnatural paleness
  A. Plausible B. Exaggerate C. Pallor D. Acquitted

_B_ 6. A short rest; a temporary suspension of a death sentence
  A. Repulsive B. Respite C. Proposition D. Matinees

_A_ 7. Horrible; wicked
  A. Heinous B. Destitute C. Imperturbable D. Adjourned

_A_ 8. Having an unknown or unacknowledged name
  A. Anonymous B. Meek C. Inevitable D. Suppressed

_B_ 9. Exactly
  A. Anonymous B. Precisely C. Dubious D. Intervened

_A_ 10. Unusual; odd
  A. Peculiar B. Inevitable C. Precisely D. Irrelevant

_C_ 11. To express disapproval or criticism
  A. Vindicated B. Promontory C. Reproach D. Suppressed

_B_ 12. Mild; gentle; submissive
  A. Respite B. Meek C. Pallor D. Inevitable

_C_ 13. Spoil; corrupt
  A. Tirade B. Imperceptibly C. Taint D. Incessant

_A_ 14. Without connections; in an unclear or unorderly manner
  A. Incoherently B. Acquitted C. Vindicated D. Obvious

_D_ 15. Arousing feelings of dislike, aversion or displeasure
  A. Zeal B. Premeditated C. Proposition D. Odious

_A_ 16. A place preserved from surrounding unpleasantness; a refuge
  A. Oasis B. Zeal C. Suppressed D. Heinous

_A_ 17. Poor; impoverished
  A. Destitute B. Odious C. Consummated D. Taint

_B_ 18. Filthy; dirty; foul; morally degraded
  A. Matinees B. Sordid C. Cordial D. Tirade

_A_ 19. Link; a means of communication between different groups
  A. Liaison B. Indignantly C. Precisely D. Zeal

_C_ 20. In such a way as to be impossible to perceive by the senses
  A. Consummated B. Liaison C. Imperceptibly D. Dubious

VOCABULARY WORKSHEET 2 - *The Stranger*

____ 1. IMPERTURBABLE   A. Can't be ruffled; unshakably calm and collected

____ 2. SUPPRESSED   B. Freed from blame or suspicion

____ 3. FURTIVE   C. Spoil; corrupt

____ 4. PECULIAR   D. Waved or flourished; displayed

____ 5. REPROACH   E. Brought to completion or fruition; fulfilled

____ 6. PALL   F. A long, angry or violent speech

____ 7. ANONYMOUS   G. Unusual; odd

____ 8. VIGIL   H. Endless; tiresome

____ 9. TAINT   I. Coffin cover

____ 10. CONSUMMATED   J. The murdering of one's parents or other close relatives

____ 11. TIRADE   K. Expressions of sympathy or comfort

____ 12. VINDICATED   L. Sneaky; stealthy

____ 13. PARRICIDE   M. Belief

____ 14. CONDOLENCES   N. Subdued; inhibited; held back

____ 15. INTERMINABLE   O. A watch

____ 16. DUBIOUS   P. Enthusiastic devotion to a cause or an ideal

____ 17. BRANDISHED   Q. To express disapproval or criticism

____ 18. ZEAL   R. Having an unknown or unacknowledged name

____ 19. INDICTMENT   S. Accusation

____ 20. CONVICTION   T. Doubtful

KEY: VOCABULARY WORKSHEET 2 - *The Stranger*

_A_	1. IMPERTURBABLE	A.	Can't be ruffled; unshakably calm and collected
_N_	2. SUPPRESSED	B.	Freed from blame or suspicion
_L_	3. FURTIVE	C.	Spoil; corrupt
_G_	4. PECULIAR	D.	Waved or flourished; displayed
_Q_	5. REPROACH	E.	Brought to completion or fruition; fulfilled
_I_	6. PALL	F.	A long, angry or violent speech
_R_	7. ANONYMOUS	G.	Unusual; odd
_O_	8. VIGIL	H.	Endless; tiresome
_C_	9. TAINT	I.	Coffin cover
_E_	10. CONSUMMATED	J.	The murdering of one's parents or other close relatives
_F_	11. TIRADE	K.	Expressions of sympathy or comfort
_B_	12. VINDICATED	L.	Sneaky; stealthy
_J_	13. PARRICIDE	M.	Belief
_K_	14. CONDOLENCES	N.	Subdued; inhibited; held back
_H_	15. INTERMINABLE	O.	A watch
_T_	16. DUBIOUS	P.	Enthusiastic devotion to a cause or an ideal
_D_	17. BRANDISHED	Q.	To express disapproval or criticism
_P_	18. ZEAL	R.	Having an unknown or unacknowledged name
_S_	19. INDICTMENT	S.	Accusation
_M_	20. CONVICTION	T.	Doubtful

VOCABULARY JUGGLE LETTER REVIEW GAME CLUES - *The Stranger*

SCRAMBLED	WORD	CLUE
DACEQTUTI	ACQUITTED	Freed from a charge or accusation
DAOJRUDEN	ADJOURNED	Suspended until a later stated time
USOMYNONA	ANONYMOUS	Having an unknown or unacknowledged name
ATTSHIE	ATHEIST	One who does not believe in God
DEHISDNARB	BRANDISHED	Waved or flourished; displayed
OCCELNSOEDN	CONDOLENCES	Expressions of sympathy or comfort
MESDAMNOCUT	CONSUMMATED	Brought to completion or fruition; fulfilled
NOCCIVNOIT	CONVICTION	Belief
LUVNOCNIOS	CONVULSION	An intense involuntary muscular contraction; violent turmoil
LAIDROC	CORDIAL	Warm and sincere; friendly
ITTESDETU	DESTITUTE	Poor; impoverished
OSIUDUB	DUBIOUS	Doubtful
EGRGXAETAE	EXAGGERATE	To represent as greater than is actually the case; overstate
IERYF	FIERY	Burning; hot; fire-like
RUFEVIT	FURTIVE	Sneaky; stealthy
SOUNIHE	HEINOUS	Horrible; wicked
CREPIMPELBTIY	IMPERCEPTIBLY	In such a way as to be impossible to perceive by the senses
LBAEMIPREBRUT	IMPERTURBABLE	Can't be ruffled; unshakably calm and collected
CBELMLPAIA	IMPLACABLE	Impossible to please
CANTSINES	INCESSANT	Continuous without interruption
CINHRONEEYLT	INCOHERENTLY	Without connections; in an unclear or unorderly manner
DINTCINETM	INDICTMENT	Accusation
YNTIGLINNDA	INDIGNANTLY	With anger aroused by something unjust
LETIVNEBAI	INEVITABLE	Unavoidable; impossible to prevent
RETINNIMELBA	INTERMINABLE	Endless; tiresome
DENEVRETNI	INTERVENED	Came between
RIRLEEVNAT	IRRELEVANT	Unrelated to the matter at hand
SIAILNO	LIAISON	Link; a means of communication between different groups
TAMNIESE	MATINEES	Afternoon (theater) performances
EKEM	MEEK	Mild; gentle; submissive
AISSO	OASIS	A place preserved from surrounding unpleasantness; a refuge
SVOOUBI	OBVIOUS	Easily seen or understood

Stranger Vocabulary Review Game Clue Sheet Continued

SOUIOD	ODIOUS	Arousing feelings of dislike, aversion or displeasure
LALP	PALL	Coffin cover
ROLALP	PALLOR	Extreme or unnatural paleness
RARPICIED	PARRICIDE	The murdering of one's parents or other close relatives
CEPRLIUA	PECULIAR	Unusual; odd
LAPUSBILE	PLAUSIBLE	Believable
REPSICYEL	PRECISELY	Exactly
DERDATTIEMEP	PREMEDITATED	Planned beforehand
MOONYORTRP	PROMONTORY	High ridge of land or rock jutting into the water
PITINOSOORP	PROPOSITION	Proposal; a plan suggested for approval
RAHPECOR	REPROACH	To express disapproval or criticism
PLUREVIES	REPULSIVE	Tending to repel or drive off; causing aversion
PETISER	RESPITE	A short rest; a temporary suspension of a death sentence
WINSYE	SINEWY	Stringy and tough; lean and muscular
DRISOD	SORDID	Filthy; dirty; foul; morally degraded
RDESSEPUPS	SUPPRESSED	Subdued; inhibited; held back
NAITT	TAINT	Spoil; corrupt
DATIRE	TIRADE	A long, angry or violent speech
UGAVE	VAGUE	Not clearly expressed; not distinct
ILIVG	VIGIL	A watch
CINVADTIDE	VINDICATED	Freed from blame or suspicion
ELAZ	ZEAL	Enthusiastic devotion to a cause or an ideal